# Identity Problems in the Facebook Era

## Daniel Trottier

D0080720

How have new social media altered how individuals present themselves? What dilemmas have they introduced? In the age of Facebook, Twitter and other forms of instant communication, individuals are losing (or relinquishing) control over their personal information. Trottier provides a trenchant analysis of the paradoxes of privacy and the presentation of self in the early 21st century. This book is ideal for courses in Sociology, Media Studies and Communication.

**Daniel Trottier** is a Postdoctoral Fellow in Social and Digital Media at the Communication and Media Research Institute (CAMRI), University of Westminster, London. His research considers the social consequences of digital media, with an emphasis on surveillance and policing.

**University Readers**
Reading Materials Evolved.

**THE SOCIAL ISSUES COLLECTION™**

**Routledge**
Taylor & Francis Group

# Framing 21st Century Social Issues

The goal of this new, unique Series is to offer readable, teachable "thinking frames" on today's social problems and social issues by leading scholars. These are available for view on http://routledge.customgateway.com/routledge-social-issues.html.

For instructors teaching a wide range of courses in the social sciences, the Routledge *Social Issues Collection* now offers the best of both worlds: originally written short texts that provide "overviews" to important social issues *as well as* teachable excerpts from larger works previously published by Routledge and other presses.

As an instructor, click to the website to view the library and decide how to build your custom anthology and which thinking frames to assign. Students can choose to receive the assigned materials in print and/or electronic formats at an affordable price.

## Available

**Body Problems**
Running and Living Long in a Fast-Food Society
Ben Agger

**Sex, Drugs, and Death**
Addressing Youth Problems in American Society
Tammy Anderson

**The Stupidity Epidemic**
Worrying About Students, Schools, and America's Future
Joel Best

**Empire Versus Democracy**
The Triumph of Corporate and Military Power
Carl Boggs

**Contentious Identities**
Ethnic, Religious, and Nationalist Conflicts in Today's World
Daniel Chirot

**The Future of Higher Education**
Dan Clawson and Max Page

**Waste and Consumption**
Capitalism, the Environment, and the Life of Things
Simonetta Falasca-Zamponi

**Rapid Climate Change**
Causes, Consequences, and Solutions
Scott G. McNall

**The Problem of Emotions in Societies**
Jonathan H. Turner

**Outsourcing the Womb**
Race, Class, and Gestational Surrogacy in a Global Market
France Winddance Twine

**Changing Times for Black Professionals**
Adia Harvey Wingfield

# Identity Problems in the Facebook Era

Daniel Trottier

University of Westminster

Routledge
Taylor & Francis Group

NEW YORK AND LONDON

First published 2014
by Routledge
711 Third Avenue, New York, NY 10017

Simultaneously published in the UK
by Routledge
2 Park Square, Milton Park, Abingdon, Oxon OX14 4RN

*Routledge is an imprint of the Taylor & Francis Group, an informa business*

©2014 Taylor & Francis

The right of Daniel Trottier to be identified as author of this work has been asserted by him in accordance with sections 77 and 78 of the Copyright, Designs and Patents Act 1988.

All rights reserved. No part of this book may be reprinted or reproduced or utilized in any form or by any electronic, mechanical, or other means, now known or hereafter invented, including photocopying and recording, or in any information storage or retrieval system, without permission in writing from the publishers.

**Trademark notice:** Product or corporate names may be trademarks or registered trademarks, and are used only for identification and explanation without intent to infringe.

*Library of Congress Cataloging in Publication Data*
Trottier, Daniel.
    Identity problems in the Facebook era / by Daniel Trottier.
    pages cm. — (Framing 21st century social issues)
    Includes bibliographical references and index.
    1. Online social networks. 2. Online identities. 3. Identity (Psychology).
    4. Internet—Social aspects. I. Title.
    HM742.T767 2012
    006.7'54—dc23
    2013021502

ISBN: 978-0-415-64345-0 (pbk)
ISBN: 978-1-203-07009-3 (ebk)

Typeset in Garamond and Gill Sans
by EvS Communication Networx, Inc.

**University Readers (www.universityreaders.com):** Since 1992, University Readers has been a leading custom publishing service, providing reasonably priced, copyright-cleared, course packs, custom textbooks, and custom publishing services in print and digital formats to thousands of professors nationwide. The Routledge Custom Gateway provides easy access to thousands of readings from hundreds of books and articles via an online library. The partnership of University Readers and Routledge brings custom publishing expertise and deep academic content together to help professors create perfect course materials that are affordable for students.

# Contents

꩜

# Series Foreword

The early years of the 21st century have been a time of paradoxes. Growing prosperity and the growth of the middle classes in countries such as Brazil, China, India, Russia and South Africa have been accompanied by climate change, environmental degradation, labor exploitation, gender inequalities, state censorship of social media, governmental corruption, and human rights abuses. Sociologists offer theories, concepts, and analytical frames that enable us to better understand the challenges and cultural transformations of the 21st century. How can we generate new forms of collective knowledge that can help solve some of our local, global, and transnational problems?

We live in a world in which new communication technologies and products such as cell phones, iPads, and new social media such as Facebook, Google, and Skype have transformed online education, global communication networks, local and transnational economies, facilitated revolutions such as the "Arab Spring," and generated new forms of entertainment, employment, protest, and pleasure. These social media have been utilized by social justice activists, political dissidents, educators, entrepreneurs, and multinational corporations. They have also been a source of corporate deviance and government corruption used as a form of surveillance that threatens democracy, privacy, creative expression, and political freedoms.

The goal of this series is to provide accessible and innovative analytical frames that examine a wide range of social issues including social media whose impact is local, global, and transnational. Sociologists are ideally poised to contribute to a global conversation about a range of issues such as the impact of mass incarceration on local economies, medical technologies, health disparities, violence, torture, transnational migration, militarism, and the AIDS epidemic.

The books in this series introduce a wide range of analytical frames that dissect and discuss social problems and social pleasures. These books also engage and intervene directly with current debates within the social sciences over how best to define, rethink, and respond to the social issues that characterize the early 21st century. The contributors to this series bring together the works of classical sociology into dialogue with contemporary social theorists from diverse theoretical traditions including but not limited to feminist, Marxist, and European social theory.

Readers do not need an extensive background in academic sociology to benefit from these books. Each book is student-friendly in that we provide glossaries of terms for the uninitiated that appear in bold in the text. Each chapter ends with questions for further thought and discussion. The books are the ideal level for undergraduates because they are accessible without sacrificing a theoretically sophisticated and innovative analysis.

This is the fourth year of our Routledge Social Issues Book series. Ben Agger was the former editor of this series during its first three years. These books explore contemporary social problems in ways that introduce basic sociological concepts in the social sciences, cover key literature in the field, and offer original diagnoses. Our series includes books on a broad range of topics including climate change, consumption, eugenics, torture, surrogacy, gun violence, the Internet, and youth culture.

This book by Daniel Trottier on digital stigma and exposure on social media offers an insightful and much-needed analysis of the perils to privacy for those who regularly use online social media. Trottier provides a nuanced analysis of the paradoxes of online communication. It is both a source of pleasure and a potential source of discipline and punishment. It is place where privacy can no longer be taken for granted. This book is ideal for courses on social problems, sociology of culture, social justice, and social theory.

France Winddance Twine
*Series Editor*

# Preface

Social media and mobile devices are platforms for interpersonal communication. Many users routinely share mundane and profound moments through these technologies. After submitting personal information to sites like Facebook, some of these users face a considerable social problem: stigma. Digital media enable users to talk about themselves—and their peers—to vast and imperceptible audiences (boyd 2008b). As a consequence, users broadcast personal details to an extent they may not anticipate. Tracking and removing this information is difficult once it is online, and it can potentially harm users' reputations. Even if they intend to present themselves in a particular way in a limited context, the contextual convergence that makes social media "social" complicates this process. Personal information that users want to keep in one context can easily leak (Lyon 2001) elsewhere. Such leaks can contribute to stigma, resulting in discrimination, damaged reputations, and other social harm.

Stigma is not a new social problem. **Erving Goffman,** the author of *Stigma,* published in 1963, defined **stigma** as personal attributes that can discredit an individual if discovered. Goffman explored this topic long before Facebook and other digital media. However, the emergence of these platforms forces a reconsideration of stigma and its social consequences. When the Internet first entered the domestic sphere, users were able to construct identities that were "anonymous, multiple and fragmented" (Kennedy 2006: 859). Yet the growing popularity of social and digital media means that users are held accountable to how they appear online. Identity "play" has given way to identity management, as well as crisis management. This book introduces a range of themes and concepts that address social problems relating to information and communication technologies, with an emphasis on stigma and spoiled identities on digital media. In addition to micro-sociological theories, this book incorporates contemporary work on digital media culture with recent examples of spoiled identities online. This material is organized along the line of argument that user activity on digital media amplifies problems common to face-to-face sociality.

# Acknowledgments

This project would not be possible without the support of my friends, family, and colleagues. I am especially grateful for Ben Agger's support and enthusiasm during the inception of this project, as well as France Winddance Twine's guidance towards its completion. Stephen Rutter and Margaret Moore ensured that editing and production were handled to the utmost degree. It has been a privilege to collaborate with them. Finally, I would like to thank the two anonymous reviewers for their detailed and constructive feedback.

# 1: Introducing Spoiled Identities Online: Digital Stigma in the 21st Century

～～✕～～

In 2010, Tyler Clementi and Dharun Ravi were paired as roommates in their freshman year at Rutgers University. They were both 18 years old. Having met Clementi online before living together, Ravi began to scrutinize his online presence, discovering what he believed were stigmatizing details about Clementi's sexual orientation. Using his computer's webcam, he recorded a video of Clementi being intimate with another man in their shared dorm room. Ravi streamed this video over the Internet, and invited his peers on Twitter to watch the video. Clementi was still coming to terms with the public expression of his sexual identity. This unwanted exposure upset him profoundly, and soon after he took his own life.

Media accounts point to several factors contributing to Clementi's suicide, including a homophobic culture on his campus, the emergence of cyber-bullying and the lack of a safe space for young people to negotiate their sexuality (NPR 2010; Spaulding 2010; Parker 2012). In addition, we can consider Ravi's use of digital media to publicize sensitive personal details. The social harm described above is not a product of **digital media**. Yet digital media, and **social media** like Twitter and Facebook in particular, enable a contemporary social problem: **digital stigma**. This refers to when sensitive personal details are made public through online platforms, resulting in negative affect, a compromised **reputation** and persistent discrimination. An individual's reputation is socially important in a way that cannot be overstated. Daniel Solove remarks that reputation "can be a key dimension of our self, something that affects the very core of our identity" (2007a: 31). Individuals may upload information about themselves without anticipating the consequences of that exposure. They may also upload information in one setting, and that information may leak elsewhere. For example, the contents of a confidential email may be copied onto a public Facebook page. In other cases, such as with Clementi and Ravi, users may upload information about their peers.

Digital stigma is a product of digital media culture, as people use platforms like Facebook to share personal information. To be clear, the social impact and relevance of digital media is linked to users' behavior on sites like Facebook, and less with the algorithms and hardware that make up these services. For instance, Facebook's recent valuation of US$67.8 billion (Satell 2013) is based on the efforts of more than a billion users, who upload over 25 billion pieces of personal information per month (Zwilling 2013). One social consequence that can become a problem occurs when this information identifies someone as belonging to a group or possessing an attribute (such as sexual orientation) that they do not want to be made publicly available. If this identification harms their reputation, their well-being, and their opportunities, it becomes a social stigma that must be managed. User practices on digital media transform sites like Facebook into platforms where stigmatizing information can be easily distributed.

Digital media are devices and software that people use to send and receive information. Social media, a subset of digital media, are platforms where users are expected to make connections with other users (whom they may or may not know beyond the platform), and to share personal details. These platforms are designed to make their content visible. Following default privacy settings on platforms like Facebook and Twitter, they publicize personal details to peers and strangers alike. On these platforms users build an audience for the details that they upload, or that others post about them. The average Facebook user has 229 friends (Pew 2012), and the average Twitter user has 208 followers (Beevolve 2012). Yet if users follow the default privacy settings, anyone with an Internet connection can access this information. And that audience can forward their personal details to an even broader audience, for example, by uploading it to another platform. Social life is more visible for digital media users who follow default privacy settings and regularly provide personal information.

Digital stigma is a serious concern for users whose lives and reputations have been harmed. However, the prevalence and social impact of digital media requires caveats when discussing this social problem. First, not everyone uses Facebook, iPhones or other digital media. These platforms and devices have become popular, but even a total of one billion Facebook users reveals that the majority of individuals—including 56 percent of North Americans (Socialbakers 2013a)—have not signed on. Moreover, those who are online may not be active. If 618 million use Facebook at least once a day (Facebook 2013), around 40 percent of users are inactive.

However, those who are excluded still risk online exposure. What harmed Clementi was not information that he uploaded, but what his roommate uploaded. Furthermore, some users turn to digital media in order to stigmatize strangers. Consider the website *PeopleofWalmart.com*, a site launched in 2009 where users can share pictures of patrons at the retail chain. These strangers are stigmatized on the basis of their appearance and behavior. On this site, Walmart's patrons are subject to ridicule by their tech-savvy peers.

Second, being a digital media user does not inevitably lead to digital stigma. For example, some users are well acquainted with Facebook's privacy settings and routinely update them. Yet privacy settings are continually revised as the interface is revised, and thus regular users have to maintain a vigilant familiarity with these modifications. A Facebook user who hides her sexual orientation from her family and co-workers may still participate in discussions about sexual identity on this platform. However, changes to the privacy settings may allow her family to read these discussions. Other users will avoid posting such details, but may still monitor personal details their peers post about them.

Third, there is variation in how individuals cope with stigma. Even if all users have something to hide (cf. Solove 2007b), embarrassing anecdotes do not result in the same burden as belonging to a persecuted racial or ethnic community. On the one hand, the shame that often accompanies stigma is a subjective affect, and individuals will cope with the same stigma in different ways. Yet digital stigma's impact is also determined by social categories including age, race, gender, sexual orientation, and socio-economic status. It is beyond the scope of this book to determine who is most vulnerable to digital stigma, but we can speculate that longstanding discrepancies in power, capital, and visibility may be reproduced online (cf. Gandy 2009).

## Facebook and Digital Media Culture: A Brief Overview

Digital stigma must be understood as it occurs in a specific cultural and historical context. Chapter 2 considers this culture in some detail, yet we can briefly consider Facebook as an exemplar. When Facebook was launched in 2004, college students used the service to communicate with their peers. Two years later, it became available to the general public, including the parents and employers of these early adopters. Advertising schemes followed in 2007, with marketers and brand managers forging a corporate presence on this platform (Trottier 2013). Law enforcement agencies now use it to gather "open-source intelligence" following riots and other criminal events (Omand, Bartlett, and Miller 2012). This development suggests that Facebook's administrators deliberately repurpose users' personal details, such that unanticipated exposure is a common outcome. Chapter 3 considers sociological perspectives toward the impact of such platforms.

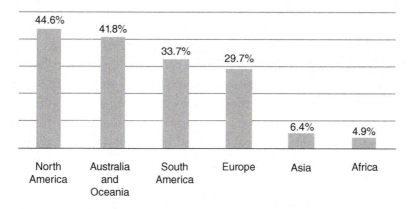

*Figure 1.1* Facebook Penetration Rate by Continent
*Source:* Socialbakers.com 2012

Facebook is integrated into the lives of a significant segment of the European and North American population. Fifty-three percent of Americans and Canadians as well as 30 percent of Europeans have an account (Socialbakers 2013b). Yet that means that 70 percent of Europeans are not on this platform. We can also consider countries like India, Russia and Pakistan, where adoption rates hover around 5 percent, as well as entire continents like Asia and Africa, where rates are 6.5 and 5 percent, respectively. Within the United States, the majority (58 percent) of Facebook users are female. This is a pattern that is repeated on most platforms, with the exception of LinkedIn (Hampton et al. 2011). Nearly half (49 percent) of Facebook users are 35 or younger, and only a quarter are 50 or older. The vast majority of users (78 percent) identify as white. Those who identify as Black or Hispanic each correspond to 9 percent of all users. Facebook's legacy as a college service remains, as 69 percent of its users have pursued higher education.

The above figures present a composite image of the typical Facebook user as a young white college student. However, there is some variance among users, which in turn shapes their experiences with digital stigma. A 20-year-old college student in the United States is not likely to upload the same type of information as a 50-year-old executive in Singapore. Indeed, a user's experience on Facebook is egocentric because it is shaped by their immediate social network (boyd and Ellison 2007). The kinds of digital stigma users may face—and the repercussions of this stigma—vary significantly. As well, those who do not fit the mold of the white college-educated user are less likely to have accounts on these sites. Facebook is not the only social media platform available to users, and social media are not the only means for digital stigma. Yet this snapshot of Facebook's user base supports the notion that being visible online is situated within a broader digital culture where marginalized communities largely remain excluded.

## Erving Goffman, Dramaturgy, and Stigma

Academics have begun to consider the social impact of digital stigma. Some scholars have focused on how users' sense of privacy is compromised because of the way they collectively adopt digital media (boyd 2008a; Trottier 2012a). Others have considered the introduction of these technologies to different social spheres, and observed that they can harm the reputations of those employed within an institution (Beer and Burrows 2007). Scholarship on social interactions also offers insight into the dynamics of identity and reputation construction, and how digital media might complicate these processes. In particular, Erving Goffman's work speaks to the problem of spoiled identities online.

Goffman, born in Alberta, Canada in 1922, studied sociology and anthropology at the University of Toronto before earning his PhD at the University of Chicago in 1953. His research examined a range of phenomena, including mental asylums (1961), interactions among members of a remote island community (1959), and the way street hustlers micro-manage their victims (1952). These topics are united by his longstanding focus on micro-level interactions and their broader relevance for social life. Goffman suggested that our understanding of society is supported by these interactions. Interaction refers to how people exchange information with each other, as well as how these exchanges collectively contribute to—and sometimes contest—our social world. Goffman described social interactions as a kind of theatrical performance. His **dramaturgical** framework contends that we perform numerous roles in our everyday life (Goffman 1959). Goffman stressed the societal importance of these performances, and mapped the locations where roles were managed and executed. Just like an actual theater, **front stages** are spaces where social performances take place. These performances are maintained in **back stages**. Whereas front stages are the public spaces where we express ourselves to the world, back stages are concealed spaces where we can temporarily suspend these performances. These locations are often quite tangible. For example, consider the typical spatial arrangement in the retail sector. Customers enter the front stage, where the staff flatters them in order to make a sale. Back stage in the break room, employees drop their performance, complain about customers, and strategize new sales techniques.

These performances might be laborious in the retail sector. Yet this effort is a more general condition of social life. As social actors, we might not always enjoy the roles we play, yet we recognize their importance for social functioning. Collectively, they contribute to a kind of framing of social life, or what W. I. Thomas called the "definition of situation" (1923: 42). Social roles are the principal means by which we convey information to others. We pick specific scenes, roles, and scripts to express ourselves. Without this information, making sense of a given situation—and our role within that situation—would be daunting. People announce their roles through social information. This can be explicitly **given** away, when people make verbal or other explicit statements. Yet we communicate through less obvious ways when we "give off" nonverbal cues. Information that is **given off** such as body language may seem less deliberate, but these cues can be just as important when delivering a social performance. Even performances in the so-called back stage follow scripts and protocols. They only appear more authentic because they are juxtaposed against front stage performances (Meyrowitz 1990: 70; Giddens 1984: 124–5).

Social life is complex because we simultaneously perform multiple roles, such as student, employee, sibling, and spouse. In addition, we also serve as the **audience** to other people's performances. The importance of an audience cannot be overstated, as all performances require them for validation. Terms such as role and performance might give the impression that dramaturgy is focused on surface-level displays. Yet for Goffman, these performances are fundamental to social functioning, and for individuals to fit in their social context. We are continuously assessed by our most recent performance, and there are plenty of opportunities to ruin them. Failed social performances are embarrassing in a way that individuals may know all too intimately. To say that we die of embarrassment when we botch a public speech may be an embellishment. Yet it also conveys deep-seated feelings of regret and shame (Scheff 2006), because our individual self-assessment is linked to our perception of how others assess us (Cooley 1922).

Our reputations are built and harmed on the basis of the information that we convey. Audiences assess our verbal and non-verbal cues. Sometimes our performances fail to live up to the roles we feel socially obliged to adopt (Mead 1934). Quite often, we give off information that compromises the performance, as well as the reputation we are trying to cultivate. Stigma refers to personal information that can damage an individual's performance and reputation. Goffman distinguishes between three kinds of stigma: abominations of the body, blemishes of character, and tribal stigma (1963: 14). The first two refer to perceived physical and personality defects, respectively. The third refers to a group, community, or category to which the individual belongs. I contend that users' adoption of digital media augments the display of stigmatizing features. Stigma is a broad concept, and stigmatizing information ranges from minor details to major identifiers. Further, the consequences range from mild embarrassment to life-compromising shame. As Goffman indicates, people tend to think of stigmatized individuals as "less than human" (ibid.: 15). It is through stigma that discrimination and inequality are manifest at the micro-social level.

A visible stigma can endanger a person's performance. Returning to the retail example, an employee may take steps to hide his recent weight gain. A customer may want to conceal that she is in severe debt. A manager, whose physical appearance allows, may choose to hide his religious, ethnic, or national origins. These stigmas risk interrupting the performances these actors are trying to uphold. Yet performances can be even more abstract, and the role of "citizen" or "woman" can be questioned as a result of stigmatizing details that social actors continuously manage. It bears noting that social actors are heavily invested in collaboratively maintaining social order, including maintaining one's own face and supporting the self-presentation and face of others (Goffman 1967). Malice among social actors is uncommon, as individuals do not typically seek to embarrass one another. When it does occur, it is often a result of an accidental social gaffe, such as the misuse of a new technology.

Concealing personal information is a common practice in both face-to-face and mediated settings. While some social groups are more vulnerable than others, all social actors have something to hide, as there is no such thing as an "unblushing" person (Goffman 1963: 128). Despite the benefits of living in public online (which can only be addressed in a cursory manner in this book), users require the right to withhold personal information. If virtually any social actor has stigmatizing attributes, and a failed social performance can provoke embarrassment, social life relies on the successful performance of roles. When a stigma may compromise a role, social actors attempt **passing** in order to sustain the impression that they in fact do not possess stigmatizing features. Passing refers to conditions of information control where "the stigma is nicely invisible and known only to the person who possesses it, who tells no one" (Goffman 1963: 92). Passing is a common strategy in situations where social actors uphold a shared reality by concealing and implicitly denying the existence of stigma.

Social actors hide discrediting information because they do not want to be discovered by individuals, but also by institutions or governments. This desire relates to **privacy**, a social value that is complicated by the migration of social life online. Nissenbaum identifies privacy as contextual integrity, or "a right to appropriate flow of personal information" (2009: 127). Social media users might post personal details online, but they maintain a right to not share all their information with everybody. Being able to determine what personal information they wish to communicate is a standard feature of social life (Westin 1967). In other words, secrecy and secrets are socially important. As stated above, social actors are invested in maintaining a collective understanding of the roles they perform. Yet some individuals do attempt to breach these roles. Someone who suspects their spouse has a gambling addiction may actively discredit and disrupt their front stage performance. Likewise, various organizations and institutions, including government branches (Lyon 2007; Dandeker 1990) have an interest in discovering personal details that citizens would prefer to conceal. Not only can stigma occasionally be sought out, but the consequences can go beyond embarrassment. Social regimes rely on categorization to make sense of the world (Bowker and Star 1999), and membership of an undesirable group can harm an individual's life chances (Gandy 1993).

## From Stigma to Digital Stigma

A **spoiled identity** is harmful in a rural community or small town, where one cannot hide their tarnished reputation. Yet the stigmatized resident may be able to relocate to another town, or seek anonymity in a larger city. This kind of escape is not as easy with digital media. Scholars commenting on Goffman's work suggest that information flows, rather than physical locations, shape social situations (Meyrowitz 1990: 88). From this perspective, digital media are configured in ways that allow different kinds of self-expression and visibility (Papacharissi 2009). Situations and definitions can be expressed and contested on new media. Mediated spaces are an extension of— rather than a rupture from—face-to-face sociality. Personal information travels across fiber-optic cable and 4G networks. It can be stored indefinitely on remote servers, and search engines as well as smart algorithms augment their visibility. According to Solove, "[a]s social reputation-shaping practices such as gossip and shaming migrate to the Internet, they are being transformed in significant ways. Information that was once scattered, forgettable, and localized is becoming permanent and searchable" (2007a: 4).

Social media's ubiquitous presence in some users' lives heightens the risk that their secrets are exposed to an immeasurable audience. Consider a digital media user's attempts to hide a physical defect. The Internet was envisioned as an alternative to the physical world, and not being bound to one's embodied identity had therapeutic potential (Turkle 1995). However, as we shall see, the body now features prominently online. Abominations of the body are more difficult to manage when digital media users take photographs of social events and post them online. Blemishes of character are also a problem on digital media. Not only are words and actions recorded and retained, but other people's opinions are an inescapable feature of living online. Regardless of their peers' intentions, users are evaluated based on virtual company that they keep (Jernigan and Mistree 2009). Tribal stigma can also become public, as so many tribes have an online presence. Ethnic (Nakamura 2002) and religious (Cheong et al. 2009) background is explicitly and implicitly present online, along with all the prejudices that target these categories.

The culture surrounding digital media complicates users' attempts to maintain distinctions between social contexts. Understood in a biographical manner, stigmatizing details from one life stage may leak into another stage. Chapter IV considers this issue in greater detail. Managing an online reputation is challenging, and several businesses claim to have a solution to this challenge. *Reputation.com* is a web-based company that specializes in digital stigma, offering customers an opportunity to rectify their online presence. They locate content linked to a client's identity, and allow clients to sanitize this content. They claim that "[n]o one asks people for job references or background information anymore, they ask Google. And if your name turns up in news reports, legal filings, embarrassing party photos, or other questionable material, you're likely to get passed over" (Reputation 2012). Whether or not companies like *Reputation.com* are able to fix this social problem is a separate discussion. However, their prevalence suggests that digital media users are compelled to cope with stigma, a point that is further explored in Chapter V.

If all the world's a stage, then living online has profoundly changed the conditions of that stage. We can briefly consider some of these changes. First, the distinction between front and back stage is less evident on digital media. Goffman referred to the back stage as "places where the camera is not focused at the moment or all places out of range of 'live' microphones" (1959: 121). Yet avoiding exposure is difficult when so many devices are equipped with cameras and microphones. Social interactions and transactions are increasingly mediated. Online spaces used to be framed as a refuge from the real world. Yet the ubiquity of social media in some users' lives means that abstaining from these platforms may more effectively shield them from social exposure. For Goffman, the stage was a situated concept. A social actor was always performing, and the risk of being discredited was ever-present. Yet this risk was contained and contextualized. In contrast, digital stigma can go **viral**, and spread rapidly to an entire social network. In addition to the stage, users have less control over their audience. A casual performance with an intimate audience can go public if a member of that audience uploads evidence of a social gaffe. Because of this kind of global spread, users face a heightened risk that their performance can be taken out of context (boyd 2008a). Information that is appropriate in one context can be devastating if it leaks elsewhere.

Social and digital media are normative spaces. These norms extend from broader social values, but they also contain their own implicit norms that are dynamic and platform-specific (McLaughlin and Vitak 2012). Users' social expectations manage how they are employed. Violating social norms is an ongoing risk, in part due to changing user cultures. Most users are aware of these risks. They are cautious when uploading content, often relying on specific criteria to determine whether this content is fit for public consumption. One young user states that "[a]nything that you wouldn't want your parents to know isn't something that should be on the Internet" (Trottier 2012a: 327). And if someone posts an image or message that harms their own reputation, many users believe that they have nobody to blame but themselves. Yet this assumption is problematic. As seen above, a user's reputation is often beyond their immediate control. Furthermore, a user cannot be expected to always be vigilant, and they may occasionally drop their guard. This is the problem with social media: they are typically present in multiple facets of users' lives (boyd 2008a). For many users, social media are always accessible, even when an abundance of alcohol or a lack of sleep compromises their judgment. While not all users share the same reasons to worry about digital stigma, social embarrassment and other forms of harm remain a possible outcome.

## DISCUSSION QUESTIONS

1. Our social performances are made up of explicit information that we give, and less obvious information that we give off. Is this distinction reproduced on Facebook, or is all information online deliberately given?
2. To describe stigma as a condition of everyday life suggests that individuals are always at risk of social embarrassment. Is social life really this risky?
3. Stigmatizing details may be distributed on digital media. Does this actually make it more difficult to manage, or are users getting better at managing their reputations online?
4. Goffman's approach to stigma treats embarrassment and shame as explicitly harmful. However, is it possible to consider shame as an emotion that is socially beneficial?

# II:  Between Y2K and Web 2.0: The Late Web, Social Convergence, and Digital Stigma

~~~×~~~

This chapter focuses on approaches to stigma and reputation management that are tied to the Internet's emergence in popular consciousness. These approaches are rooted in a **postmodern** notion of the self and society that questions the progressive nature of modern society in order to consider alternatives, such as the possibility that online spaces could be an escape from stigma. This chapter draws on scholarly works and popular culture that anticipated the early web's social consequences. The now-famous New Yorker cartoon claiming that "on the internet, nobody knows you're a dog" (Cartoonbank 2011) summarizes the approach described in the first part of this chapter. It then considers the technological and socio-cultural developments that occurred since the Internet's initial growth, and how these changes call into question earlier assumptions about the Internet and reputation. A loose set of developments united under the banner of "Web 2.0" is then considered. Not only do new online services situate and identify users, but the adoption of these services by so many users means that the distinction between online and offline is blurring, notably with their emphasis on producing and broadcasting personal content. Users are increasingly visible on platforms once associated with anonymity and identity play.

Facebook CEO Mark Zuckerberg claims that sharing personal details online has become "the norm" (Johnson 2010). Yet this development was not inevitable. When the Internet was introduced to the domestic sphere, its popularity was based on an entirely different vision. Identities online were typically anonymous, fragmented, and fluid (Kennedy 2006; Rheingold 1993), providing users with a greater sense of freedom and autonomy when compared to the social convergence that characterizes social media.

**The Early Web and Identity Freedom**

The individuals who conceived of the early web had a specific understanding about its role in society: it was designed for users to share information in a particular context. It first emerged as a secure means for the military to relay information (Abbate 1999). Later, universities adopted it in order to share research data. Its use shifted when entering the domestic sphere, with non-professional users now able to search and upload information pertaining to their private lives.

One of the more popular online communities in the 1980s was **Usenet**. Unlike today's social networks, Usenet was structured by topic. Users built a community based on common interests, as opposed to connecting with people they already knew (Hauben and Hauben 1997). Its members would post messages on specific subject matter, and respond to each other's messages in threads. The catchall community "**alt**" featured conversations about subcultures and alternative sexualities. Many of its members had secrets that they could not share with friends, co-workers, or loved ones. Instead, they shared information online, under a supposed guise of anonymity (Donath 1999). Users discussed sensitive and stigmatizing topics, including fetishes, mental health concerns, and abusive relationships. Users found support in each other, in part because they did not know one another (Galagher, Sproull, and Kiesler 1998). These conversations were fulfilling precisely because they had no direct bearing on the lives of those involved.

Other online venues like chat rooms, including **Internet Relay Chat** (or IRC), were platforms for discreet revelations. If a user struggled with a sensitive issue such as an eating disorder, they were probably uncomfortable discussing these issues with friends or family (Slater 1998). The mere decision to bring up such a topic meant revealing a very intimate part of themselves. Turning to venues like Usenet or IRC allowed users to broach and explore difficult, yet profoundly important topics without fear of repercussions. Moreover, they allowed people to experiment with their identity, a feature that was epitomized by the New Yorker cartoon described at the opening of this chapter. Users could test social boundaries by altering personal details like their age, their gender, or their career (Rheingold 1993). Many of these interfaces were text-based, so it was easy for a user to convince others that he was a 50-year-old homosexual from Manhattan when he was actually a 17-year-old from Missouri who was unsure about his sexuality. Users could explore unusual forms of self-expression in a safe environment.

These early web services are indicative of specific kinds of online sociality, shaped by those who oversaw their development. For these developers, the Internet was a progressive social force. Services like Usenet and IRC were an attempt toward a more expressive and accepting society. Tim Berners-Lee, inventor of the World Wide Web, elaborates on this vision:

> Perhaps I should explain where I'm coming from. I had (and still have) a dream that the web could be less of a television channel and more of an interactive sea of shared knowledge. I imagine it immersing us as a warm, friendly environment made of the things we and our friends have seen, heard, believe or have figured out. I would like it to bring our friends and colleagues closer, in that by working on this knowledge together we can come to better understandings. If misunderstandings

are the cause of many of the world's woes, then can we not work them out in cyberspace. And, having worked them out, we leave for those who follow a trail of our reasoning and assumptions for them to adopt, or correct.

(Berners-Lee 1995)

Berners-Lee envisioned the Internet as a place to bring people, including close acquaintances, together in a supportive environment where they could express themselves and understand each other. This vision merges the real-talk and identity play found in the above services with the kind of social convergence that characterizes the more recent services like Facebook. From this perspective, the Internet was supposed to have a transformative effect on users, notably how they understood and interacted with their broader social world. Stigma could be addressed directly, to everyone's benefit.

Academic perspectives at the time largely supported this vision of the early web. Sherry Turkle (1995) observed that as computers and the Internet had a more prominent role in users' lives, they were increasingly involved in how users interacted with others and understood themselves. The web could be a space for personal growth, as a result of the flexibility and anonymity that it afforded. Other scholars observed that this understanding of the web was a postmodern approach to online communication, as self-expression was not rooted in a specific offline context (Robinson 2007). However, this kind of rootless approach was often harnessed with the intention of creating a safer world for self-expression, which is a rather modernist ambition. Mark Poster considered how the Internet had the potential to be a more pluralistic and accommodating media, although he also remarked that "[p]articipation in the information superhighway and virtual reality will most likely be accessible to and culturally consonant with wealthy, white males. In these respects the media reflect the relations of force that prevail in the wider community" (1995: 47) While the novelty of the early web meant it had a transformative potential for social relations, the above quote suggests that it was more likely to reproduce existing imbalances.

One ideal underlying the early web was that dialogue between individuals could be based on ideas and reason, rather than appearance and status. Having found a venue to experiment with their identity and address sensitive topics, users were expected to communicate with each other in a way that was progressive and socially beneficial (Barbrook 2000). In a quasi-utopian sense, the Internet was framed as a break from all the constraints and risks that plagued the offline world. But even in the days of the early web, social interactions contained potential for spoiled identities. Chat rooms and discussion boards may be distinct from the outside world, but they contain norms that users can violate (Evans 2001; Powers 2003). In an example of categorical deception (Donath 1999), a forum dedicated to alternative sexualities may ostracize an individual user if it revealed that they are experimenting, and not as fully committed as other members. Social gaffes could also harm users' reputations. At the time, risks were often limited to a contextually spoiled identity, rather than a completely spoiled one. A likely outcome was that a user's reputation on a specific forum or chat room was ruined, and that they were banned from that venue (ibid.). However, when that venue was their refuge from an otherwise hostile social environment, such exclusion could be devastating.

In her research on Usenet, Donath (ibid.) distinguishes between anonymous and pseudonymous identities. The latter is disconnected from an offline identity but is still internally consistent and coherent. Too much reliance on the former could be stigmatizing, depending on the context of the online environment. Moreover, there is always the risk that the pseudonymous identity and its stigmatizing attributes could leak into the offline world. Frequenting a seemingly confidential message board for people with a sexually transmitted disease can lead to stigma if the user provides personal information on the site, or if their peers catch them browsing it. Furthermore, confidential details from the early web can resurface. In 2001, Google announced that it had acquired a company that managed Usenet archives (Google 2001). Conversations that Usenet members intended to keep in a separate context are only a Google search away.

## The Rise of Web 2.0

The Internet was designed to be a location for users to circulate personal information. In the mid-2000s, new services further actualized this vision. **Web 2.0** refers to a strategy for constructing web-based services. When the term first emerged in public discourse, it was associated with websites like Friendster, Orkut, and Myspace, all of which are social networking services that predate Facebook.

In his assessment of the transition toward Web 2.0, Tim O'Reilly suggests that: "[t]he central principle behind the success of the giants born in the Web 1.0 era who have survived to lead the Web 2.0 era appears to be this, that they have embraced the power of the web to harness collective intelligence" (2005). Web 2.0 is made up of several features, but perhaps the most crucial among them is a collective effort that comes from **user-generated content**. This refers to the extent that those who visit a site will also provide the text, images, and video that make up that site. Many contemporary sites are maintained by unaffiliated users, rather than by professional content producers. Ritzer and Jurgenson have commented on this prosumer (producer-consumer) phenomenon, where "capitalists have more difficulty controlling prosumers than producers or consumers and there is a greater likelihood of resistance on the part of prosumers" (2010: 31). A culture based on user input suggests a new model based on "free" services and "free" labor. This is a vision that renders Web 2.0 meaningful, shaping what is possible and probable within it. Although companies may relinquish some control over to users under prosumption, scholars like Fuchs (2011) and Andrejevic (2007) contend that service owners ultimately maintain control in this process, and that users are experiencing a further commoditization and exploitation of social life.

Sites that rely on user-generated content are now among the most popular on the web. Facebook, YouTube, and Twitter are ranked as the second, third, and ninth most visited sites worldwide at the time this book was written (Alexa 2012). The popularity of user-generated content has even impacted mass media, which increasingly make appeals to their audiences for input. While call-in radio shows have traditionally relied on audience members to share their opinions, many television news channels now incorporate content from Twitter in order to fill airtime (Hirsch 2008). Although such examples are indicative of mass media's reliance on free content, they also speak to the popularity of user-generated content beyond Web 2.0. The fact that users embrace these services suggests that they are drawn to information their peers give and give off, and are occasionally eager to add their own content.

Other features distinguish Web 2.0 services. First, they are typically made up of individual profiles. In most cases, a user cannot simply visit a site like Facebook; they have to build a presence there. Profiles are a kind of biographical space, where users provide information about themselves. If someone wants to gather information about a user, often the easiest way is to refer to that user's profile. For this reason, I liken the profile to a kind of dwelling (Trottier 2012b). Furthermore, most Web 2.0 services allow users to provide frequent input to supplement this presence. This is usually information that is relevant to a specific context, and so this information is authored and made available to the user's personal audience (Davis 2010). This audience is the third feature of these services: they encourage users to connect with fellow users. After all, what is the social relevance of online content if there is nobody with whom to share it?

Web 2.0 refers to locations that house user-generated content. I contend that this housing imagery is apt, since they are designed so that users can have a prolonged engagement with them. They are open-ended in their purpose, to the point they are vaguely defined by their designers. Facebook claims that they help users "keep up with friends (...) and learn more about the people they meet" (FBInfo 2012). Likewise, Twitter suggests that it will help users "[f]ind out what's happening, right now, with the people and organizations you care about" (Twitter 2012). These mission statements are fascinating in and of themselves, as companies that were inconceivable a few years ago now justify their existence as vital interpersonal resources.

Social media platforms depend on user-generated content. They are designed with the intention of being pervasive in everyday life. This ambition requires a steady influx of user-generated content. **Sharing** is a key verb in this context. Sharing can refer to any kind of content, but it is most often associated with personal information. Users are first expected to submit biographical details, and then describe their interpersonal network by connecting with peers (or providing their contact information if those peers are not already enrolled). Once this is accomplished, users are encouraged to provide a continuous stream of personal details. This focus enables users to communicate with peers. Users clearly value the interpersonal benefits of new media technologies (Ellison, Steinfield, and Lampe 2007; boyd 2010), even if these benefits are part of a persistent campaign from software, hardware, and telecommunication companies (Mosco 2004). Yet an increase in online sharing of personal information—as evidenced from the growth of services like Facebook and Twitter—can contribute to digital stigma. Companies market these services using deliberate imagery. Sharing has connotations that shape the way users perceive and adopt these services. Unlike other terms like "broadcast," "expose," or "leak," sharing suggests that the content that is uploaded is interpersonally relevant. Moreover, it implies that the intended audience is both known and trusted, as opposed to the strangers who make up the vast majority of any social media service's user base. Related stakeholders also participate in the framing of digital media as sharing. Hardware manufacturers as well as Internet and cellular service providers employ this language to sell the latest device, or the fastest connection. Sharing is a misrepresentation, as these are not simple exchanges between two acquaintances. Rather, they are mediated transactions involving servers, algorithms, and archives. Social media platforms coupled with mobile devices augment and automate the distribution of personal information on a global scale.

We may wonder what kind of self-presentation and visibility are possible—and probable—as a result of this shift. Some scholars suggest that Facebook and other services are "nonymous" (Zhao, Grasmuck, and Martin 2008). While a pseudonymous identity is internally consistent but disconnected from the offline world, the nonymous identity is anchored to "institutions, residence, or mutual friends" (ibid.: 1818). Presumably, this kind of anchored visibility means that social interactions and identity management more closely resemble what Goffman describes as presentation of self.

Web 2.0 as a concept has largely been replaced by the vaguely descriptive "social media." The term "social" is a conceptual quagmire, and a researcher could devote their career to unpacking its meaning in the context of contemporary digital media. Yet the social connectivity they offer is a germane starting point. Social media is shorthand for "social convergence media," in that these services can bring together many discrete sections of users' everyday life. danah boyd outlines this dynamic when she refers to collapsed contexts (2010). Instead of online communication removed from offline contexts, social media are often used to bridge formerly distinct contexts. And while bringing these contexts together can be framed in a positive light (imagine a party where all your friends were invited), it can also contribute to social harms that may only be apparent in retrospect. Media boundaries determine behavioral patterns, and converging media will "foster integrated behavioral patterns" (Meyrowitz 1990: 94). The act of converging formerly distinct behavioral patterns can lead to digital stigma if behavior in one context clashes with another context. Discussing mental health concerns with a therapist might be helpful, but sharing this conversation with co-workers could lead to social harm. This connectivity is framed in a broader cultural context of network sociality, where professional and personal spheres increasingly overlap (Wittel 2001). Social media sites are a means to consolidate users' social lives and identities, both of which have typically been fragmented.

The Internet used to be treated as a space that was distinct from the offline world. Now, the distinction between online and offline is largely antiquated (Jurgenson 2012a). The late web connects formerly distinct sections of users' lives. This connection is even more pervasive with the growth of the **mobile web**. By accessing the Internet on mobile devices, users can submit content to social media virtually anywhere. A user can take a picture with their phone, and immediately upload that photo to their social network. This convenience means that sharing may supersede reflecting. Davis (2010) describes a temporal buffer between reflection and presentation on social media. While users might benefit from thinking before they share, this reflection is likely contextualized with a particular audience in mind. The fact that this imagined audience might not be the entire audience suggests that social media communication can lead to digital stigma.

## DISCUSSION QUESTIONS

1. This chapter suggests that on the early web, users could share embarrassing personal details without much risk of stigma. This is no longer the case. Is this because online platforms have changed, or because more people are using the Internet, making it more likely that users are identified?
2. Social media rely on a kind of social convergence to situate all users on a social network. This can trigger embarrassment and spoiled identities when sensitive details leak into the public domain. Could users remedy this problem by using specific web services for different aspects of their lives?
3. Sites like Facebook and Twitter rely on users sharing personal information with each other. Users may forget that these sites are also businesses. Why is "sharing" so vital to their business models?

# III: Balancing Determinism and Constructionism: Understanding the Social Impact of Technologies

~~~~~

his chapter provides an overview of conflicting perspectives toward digital media technologies, with an emphasis on digital stigma. It begins with a **technological determinist** perspective that suggests new technologies have direct effects on the social world. It then considers a **social constructionist** perspective where humans inscribe values and functions into technologies. Weighing the merits of both approaches, it endorses a mutual shaping perspective. This approach contends that social actors with specific ideologies and intentions construct technologies, which in turn enable and constrain what is socially possible. Applied to digital stigma, a mutual shaping perspective contends that social media are socially meaningful as a result of digital media culture, which in turn is shaped by the kinds of information exchange that are possible on services like Facebook.

## Who to Blame: Technologies, Individuals, or Institutions?

With approximately one billion users on Facebook, and five times as many active cell phone connections (BBC 2010), digital media are present in many users' domestic spheres. The domestication of communication technologies triggers a tension "between the familiar and the strange, desire and unease, which all new technologies respectively embody and stimulate" (Silverstone and Haddon 1996: 48). Digital media may become familiar to users, but this familiarity can trigger unfamiliar conditions and unease. In 2009, a teenager sought retaliation against his sister, who revealed to his parents that he was hiding alcohol in his room. He scanned and uploaded his sister's "hook-up" list on Facebook. This handwritten list contained the names of roughly a dozen peers with whom she allegedly had sexual relations. The list included explicit details, and was likely not meant for public consumption. Not only did her friends and family see the list, but this incident also received viral exposure on digital media (Gearfuse 2009). She is now coping with the stigma of being sexually promiscuous, a label that her brother would not have to cope with had their roles been reversed. This stigma has likely tainted relations with her parents, her classmates, but also with people on the Internet whom she has never met.

This incident supports the view that digital media can harm a person's reputation, notably when it is used to publicize stigmatizing information that would otherwise remain private. The brother likely acted out of malice, with the intention to harm his sister's reputation. Yet this would not have been possible without Facebook. The brother might have been able to circulate the note without social media, but this would require more effort, and it would probably not spread to as wide an audience. Digital media's domestication means that a familiar strain of sibling rivalry, coupled with a newly familiar set of devices and software, produced a kind of social harm that is entirely unanticipated.

If we examine the history of new technologies, we discover that they are frequently linked to social problems. By virtue of what technologies allow users to do, they change the boundaries of what is possible and convenient. For instance, stalking, harassment, and fraud all occur on digital media (Topping 2012; Farrell 2012). Extending from the claim that digital media facilitate social coordination (Shirky 2008), it is arguably also easier to commit felonies online. However, earlier instances of "new" media technologies featured many of the same risks in public discourse (Mosco 2004). Prior to social media profiles, public discourse presented chat rooms as a risk to users' safety. By virtue of the way they connected users, they were linked to an elevated risk of encountering sexual predators (Microsoft 2012). We can trace this tendency even further by looking at how the domestication of the telephone was initially presented as harmful to households (Martin 1991).

Although there are tangible problems associated with any technology, there is also a lot of hype. The latter can be invoked to sell a product or a political cause. Journalists exploit a fear of technology in order to sensationalize a slow news day. Likewise, academic research is not immune from fear-mongering. Scholars may feel compelled to make a social issue appear more problematic than it actually is. For this reason, students should exercise critical thinking when approaching a so-called social problem, especially one that is linked to the latest technology.

## Technological Determinism

Whether or not it is true, many scholars contend that technologies have a direct effect on the social world. Expectations of what technologies will "do" to users are based on a technological determinist approach. This approach treats technologies, that is, hardware (devices) and software (applications), as agents of social change. By virtue of how these devices and software are designed, they are believed to have a particular social impact.

On first pass, many social issues—including climate change, traffic, and unemployment—are the result of the technologies that saturate our lives. In the case of the Internet and social media, a technological determinist approach would contend that they have specific effects on our reputations. First, they make users' personal information more public. They erode users' privacy by publicizing their most intimate secrets (Chakrabortty 2010). They expose users in unanticipated ways. These statements resonate with a contemporary digital media culture. Yet the grammar is perplexing. The fact that social media is the subject in these sentences is counter-intuitive. It implies that Facebook does something to users, as if they were coerced by software. Does blaming video games for violent outbursts (or Twitter for publicizing embarrassing ones) describe the social influence these technologies possess, or is it an attempt to find a simple explanation for a complex social problem?

Technological determinism has been criticized for several reasons. From a social scientific approach, it overlooks other factors that we will consider below. Services like Facebook shape how users' identities are presented online. However, to say that Facebook does something reduces a multivariate process to a gratifying but inaccurate blame-game. Social action does not transpire in such a straightforward manner. Furthermore, technological impacts are typically manifest when the technology in question is no longer contested or controversial (Nye 2006). In other words, technologies can more readily shape social relations when users have grown accustomed to their presence in everyday life (cf. Weiser 1991).

A technological determinist approach provides some helpful insights. In particular, it stresses that introducing a new technology involves new ways of structuring and arranging human life (Winner 1986). Moreover, specific intentions and socio-political agendas are built into new technologies. Yet this is precisely why scholars and students need to consider the point at which such values are embedded. To be clear, there is a reason to be concerned about social media and mobile phones. Yet these technologies do not render users unaccountable for their behavior. This criticism is directed against scholarly research, but also against the way technologies are represented in public discourse. This approach can enable journalists as well as marketers to overstate the social impact of a new technology. A comprehensive understanding of the impact digital media hold over users' reputations requires a more media-literate interpretation of these claims.

## Social Constructionism

Facebook and mobile phones are not to blame for digital stigma. Individuals maintain some control over their use of digital media. A social constructionist approach argues that social values shape technologies (Wacjman 1991). It stems from a broader constructionist approach to society that argues concepts such as "disease," "gender," and "aging" are products of our social upbringing. This is not to say that aging, or publicized lists of sexual acts, are merely a state of mind. Rather, the way users recognize them, the terms users employ to describe them, the beliefs users associate with them, and the measures users adopt in response to them, are based on pre-existing values and interests (Berger and Luckmann 1966).

Applied to digital stigma, a social constructionist would argue that users collectively decide to employ digital media for specific purposes, and these purposes are a product of a self-branding culture also located in reality television and party photography (Hearn 2008). Different values would result in different engagements with these technologies. For instance, LinkedIn is less associated with public displays of self-expression, and more with tightly regulated professional exchanges (Papacharissi 2009). This distinction cannot be explained by technical feature that LinkedIn holds over other social media services. Rather, both LinkedIn's designers and users have a particular vision of its purpose, and stigmatizing content is not included in that vision.

Users shape how they understand and engage with digital media. Yet the social construction of technologies also applies to how they are produced. Designers and marketers inscribe social values into a technology at a formative stage, and their intentions partly construct how users come to understand a given technology. If Facebook designers want users to share personal information, they can facilitate this process by making the open flow of this information the default setting, and then complicate privacy settings to discourage users from closing this flow (Zimmer 2008).

A social constructionist understanding of digital media addresses some of the shortcomings of technological determinism. Yet this perspective is not immune to criticism either. Whereas a technological determinist approach overstates the social impact of software and devices, social constructionism overstates the impact of social factors on technologies. It rests on a claim that individuals exercise full liberties on the social world, notably in their ability to shape and manipulate technologies. This interpretation contributes to a belief that if users encounter a problem with a technology, they can simply change it. If this were the case, what prevents users from simply establishing a digital media service that does not leak their personal details into the public eye?

## Mutual Shaping

To be clear, technologies are flexible. They are shaped by the way that human values influence their design, how they are marketed, and how they are consumed. Yet there are limits to this flexibility. And more importantly, not all individuals have the privilege of exercising this flexibility. In the case of a new mobile phone, a designer may be more influential than an early adopter, who in turn may have more influence over how it is used than a late adopter (Rohracher 2003). Our understanding of these issues is clouded by the notion of the empowered user. Because users actively participate in the media they consume, we may believe that individuals can use digital media for any purpose they desire, and that they only have themselves to blame when they encounter digital stigma. Not only will the average user cope with technological constraints, but they must also contend with social factors like peer and institutional influence over the technology in question (Boczkowski 2004). Moreover, categorical discrimination based on ethnicity, gender, and class will likely shape relations on digital media (Watkins 2009).

Most people would hesitate to identify with either of the above perspectives. Technological determinism and social constructionism are extreme positions that are diametrically opposed. A more helpful understanding of technologies is located in the center ground. A mutual shaping approach reconciles technological and social influence. From this perspective, both technology and society shape each other (e.g. Faulkner 2001). Individuals influence technologies when they design and use them, but technologies in turn shape human behavior. They place constraints on what is possible, or at least what is the most convenient way to perform a task. A commuter in Los Angeles does not necessarily need a car to travel to work, but reliance on bicycles and public transit typically becomes less likely if they have access to one. The relative ease of driving compared to the alternatives is not exactly social control, but it is enough of an influence to ensure that they may never voluntarily ride the bus to work.

A mutual shaping approach considers key actors who shape and are also shaped by technologies. A designer has a clear influence over the construction of a new device. Yet to a certain extent the device takes on a life of its own, which in turn constrains designers' and other social actors' relations to that technology. The user's behavior changes because of digital media, but they can also influence how they collectively understand digital media. This is especially true of "prosumers," who are explicitly called upon to add value to websites and devices (Ritzer and Jurgenson 2010). Less obvious actors matter as well, such as the journalist who influences how the technology is presented in the press. Yet new technologies will also shape the stories that journalists produce. Digital media in particular will even impact their ability to earn a living reporting the news (Bird 2009).

Recent scholarship offers a balanced perspective toward social media. For example, danah boyd refers to social networking sites as networked publics, which are a product of culture and technology:

> Networked publics' affordances do not dictate participants' behavior, but they do configure the environment in a way that shapes participants' engagement. In essence, the architecture of a particular environment matters and the architecture of networked publics is shaped by their affordances. The common dynamics fall out from these affordances and showcase salient issues that participants must regularly contend with when engaging in these environments.
>
> (2010: 39)

boyd carefully describes how features like friend lists and profiles reinforce a particular information architecture, and particular kinds of sharing and leaking. Likewise, Davis (2010) asserts that social media's structural affordances, including their propensity for overt communication, contextualized ambiguity, as well as a gap between identity management and identity presentation, provide users with more control over their personal information. Paying attention to deliberate features is useful, and we may apply this approach to more recent Facebook developments.

As an example of mutual shaping of digital media, consider the Facebook wall. The wall serves as the centerpiece of an individual profile. Facebook's designers created the wall to fulfill a specific purpose: to provide a mediated space where users and their peers could post messages, links, and images. They describe it as "a way to give your friends the full story of what's happening with you" (Slee 2008). Users largely followed these intentions in practice. They may also use the wall in ways that were unanticipated by designers, for instance, by posting updates from a fictional pseudonym. Yet as a result of how the wall is configured, their behavior is partly predetermined. Furthermore, the Facebook wall itself produces effects that were unanticipated in its design. For instance, the fact that a user can scroll down to the beginning of their profile means they can access nearly a decade's worth of personal information. This feature publicizes a procession of the minute details of a person's life in a way that was possibly unplanned. Once it is established, Facebook's designers may attempt to revise the wall's functioning. Yet alterations are difficult when a technology is integrated into users' lives. At the very least, users express frustrations when a technology they take for granted is modified. A striking example is the uproar whenever Facebook's developers modify the wall (Zuckerberg 2006).

Rather than treat technology and society as distinct, or conflate one with the other, a mutual shaping approach states that they "are related internally in such a way that one can speak of the technological mediation of human subjectivity and the conduct of everyday life" (Schraube 2009: 297). In this sense, technology is more than a means to an end. Rather, it opens up a field of possibilities, many of which are unanticipated. Consider the mobile phone as an example "… of the non-imagined but imaginable action of things" (ibid.: 306):

A mobile phone is a practical device, enabling a person to call a friend or be called. But it is also a product fundamentally transforming social conditions and relations. Simply the quality of being able to be carried around, unlike traditional phones, and transcending the telephone's previous temporal and spatial coordinates, fundamentally changes the situatedness of everyday experience and action, for example present/absent, public/private, near/far, concentration/distraction relations. This creates new forms of human relations to the world and self, new forms of communicating, establishing relationships, new forms of sociability and community, and so on, all highly contradictory changes in individual and social life which were not imagined when designing the device but can become apparent, imaginable, and recognizable afterwards.

(ibid.: 306)

The introduction and domestication of a new technology is linked to an ambivalence surrounding anticipated and unanticipated social effects. Non-imagined effects may contribute to stigma, yet imagined stigmatizing effects may be overstated. Technological effects include the imagined and non-imagined but imaginable, but also the probable and the possible.

Digital technologies are not simply tools for coping with specific needs. Instead, they become the principal means through which users express their identities, and communicate with others. Many users dwell in—and live through—technologies that they often take for granted. Those who study the introduction of new technologies describe a common trajectory (Nye 2006). When a new technology first goes public, there are usually several variations on the same concept. The organizations that produce these alternatives compete against one another for recognition as the dominant standard. Many readers may be old enough to remember VHS cassettes, but they likely do not remember Betamax, an alternative video-recording format. Betamax fell into obscurity in the 1980s when VHS succeeded in becoming an industry standard, much like HD-DVD fell into obscurity with the more recent ascension of Blu-ray technology. It may seem inevitable that users would come to adopt a particular video player, or social networking site. Yet it is not possible to predict which technologies will supplant their alternatives. As for Facebook, the popular press anticipates that it will either become a socially dominant platform (Mouton 2013), or will be replaced by an industry rival (Protalinski 2012). While scholars cannot predict the long-term history of a given technology, they can gain insight by studying how people describe it. I first developed a hunch that Facebook would have a long-term presence when users stopped comparing it to earlier social networking sites like Friendster and Myspace, and began talking about it in the same breath as a broader set of services like email and search engines. Not only did Facebook become a standard social media service, but the concept of social media was also elevated alongside other basic features of the Internet.

The following chapters consider how digital technologies can influence users' behavior, notably when it comes to managing potentially harmful personal information. University students who use these technologies may already have some experiences and beliefs about how digital media shape their behavior, as well as their beliefs and values. Yet a social scientific approach has to go beyond our immediate observations in order to consider the long-term effects. In other words, what happens to users' ability to manage their reputations when they come to take these technologies for granted? Life without Internet access is inconceivable for many users, in the same way that life without electricity may not seem feasible. Not only do these technologies exert influence over users' lives, but these users often disregard how they function, so long as they function. To quote Susan Leigh Star: "[t]he normally invisible quality of working infrastructure becomes visible when it breaks" (1999: 382).

Digital media have become taken for granted by many users. In addition, they pick up new functions over time. **Function creep** refers to when a technology used in a particular context is repurposed for other settings (Lyon 2001). When a technology features prominently in users' lives, it becomes easier to imagine using it for other reasons. In popular culture, baby monitors seem to be used almost exclusively to catch unfaithful spouses. This partly reflects users' intentions: if they conceive of a new solution to an old problem, they can simply attempt that solution. Yet function creep is also a product of the fact that the technology happens to be both available and familiar. The term "creep" is fitting, as users experience this repurposing as discomforting (Trottier 2012b). With social media, the fact that a service for interpersonal communication has extended into the corporate world is creepy, especially when employers use it to evaluate a job candidate's profile (Arthur 2012). Since 2006, Facebook has crept from the university to other social spheres. Chapter 4 considers the impact of this growth for digital stigma.

## DISCUSSION QUESTIONS

1.  A mutual shaping approach claims that both technologies and society hold influence over how users approach digital media. What specific cultural values have shaped the way they understand and use social media like Facebook?
2.  The more users take a particular technology for granted, the more it constrains their behavior. In what ways do mobile phones shape users' behavior?
3.  When users take digital media for granted, they might wish to consider alternatives. What kinds of alternative features and user practices for social media would be socially productive?

# IV: Digital Stigma at Different Life Stages: From the Sonogram to the Digital Grave

﹌﹏﹌

This chapter considers the extent to which digital stigma can impact those who use services like Facebook at various stages of their lives. Many parents who are familiar with digital media usher their children onto the web with videos and photographs. Likewise, users pay tribute to the recently deceased on memorial websites. Through wall posts and tagged photos, individuals speak on each other's behalf. As these services allow for long-term retention and easy public access of personal information, digital media culture complicates attempts to manage one's reputation.

Some digital media users encounter problems when managing their personal information on the Internet. Chapter II considered the emergence of a digital media culture based on sharing personal information in public, cross-contextual forums. Chapter III focused on sociological understandings of the social impact of technologies, balancing the affordances of emerging technologies against the intentions of the individuals who design and use them. These social actors are situated in a particular digital media culture, one that is partly shaped by their demographics. Facebook users are disproportionately young, white, and college-educated (Hampton et al. 2011). It bears repeating that not all users are equally vulnerable to digital stigma, nor are those who suffer from digital stigma harmed to the same degree. By considering various life stages, we attempt to understand the breadth of digital media users and the challenges that they encounter. This is by no means a comprehensive overview. Digital stigma is a nascent topic of study, and empirical data on specific populations are not yet available. What follows is a combination of existing sociological material on life stages and digital media, coupled with recent examples of spoiled identities online.

In considering digital stigma at various life stages, this chapter maintains a distinction between the possible and probable. An important caveat when critically assessing new social risks is the distinction between what could happen, and what is likely to happen. Our use of digital media is riddled with risks, which "signify a future which is to be prevented" (Beck 1992: 33). The fact that these are preventable outcomes suggests that digital stigma "are both *real* and *unreal*," and anticipating potential outcomes shapes our judgment, such that "the past loses the power to determine the present. Its place is taken by the future, thus, something non-existent, invented, fictive as the 'cause' of the current experience and action" (ibid.: 34, emphasis in original). Contemporary scholars consider whether this future risk is a legitimate concern (e.g. Boesel 2012). Just because stigmatizing content can appear online does not guarantee that it will appear, or that this content will cause social harm. Yet the kinds of exposure described below are made possible by digital media, and the culture that surrounds the design and use of these technologies.

In accounting for a diverse user population, we can consider a distinction between those who are familiar with digital media, and those who are less familiar. The term **digital native** refers to people born after 1980 who were socialized in a world with personal computers and the Internet (Jones and Shao 2011). This is not a fixed category, such that those who were born in the 1990s may not remember a time without the Internet, but also social media and mobile phones. The term digital native is meant to invoke the idea that young users are more comfortable with digital media (Tapscott 1998). Yet many who were born before the 1980s, the so-called **digital immigrants**, have also made the Internet a part of their everyday life. Taking this distinction at face value, we may suppose that older users are less likely to upload personal information on social media, in part because they are less comfortable with these platforms. However, this distinction between natives and immigrants lacks empirical grounding (Stoerger 2009), and should not be understood as an actual generation gap. It may help to replace an age-based division with one that distinguishes enthusiastic from reluctant users. Moreover, digital media users who do not consider themselves to be "computer people" may nevertheless broadcast much of their personhood online. Many have taken up Facebook profiles, reunited with old friends, and former life stages have resurfaced (Madden 2010).

A new life stage can be an opportunity to cultivate a desired social standing. In a new context, an individual can conceal stigmatizing information in an attempt to pass. A student who was bullied at high school may attempt to escape harm by moving to a new city upon graduation (cf. Goffman 1963: 79). Yet digital media culture often entails a kind of social convergence (boyd 2010; Trottier 2012a) where previously distinct contexts now intersect. If incoming college students want to know more about their roommates and classmates, they can turn to Facebook and find information about their new peers' high-school lives. Indeed, this kind of digital scrutiny allowed Ravi to stigmatize Clementi in 2010 (see Chapter I).

### Born into a Spoiled Identity

Children who are too young to speak may already have an extensive presence on digital media. We can only speculate about the issues that children born in the Facebook era will encounter. Baby photos are not always fit for public consumption, as they can reveal aspects of a person's past that they may prefer to keep private. For example, a transgender person would likely want to conceal photographs that are gendered in a way that clashes with their identity. Many parents will document the prenatal development, birth, and growth of their children (Fonio et al. 2007). The child's digital presence emerges from her parents' profiles. Milestones are documented, but baby exposure is also mundane, and details about feeding schedules and sleep habits are also broadcast. Such broadcasting has become so pervasive that a group of programmers have produced *Unbaby.me*, an online service that removes baby-related content on social media platforms. Thus, the first instance of a child's online presence is as a nuisance to be filtered out. Even if this presence is not directly stigmatizing, it may contribute to a presentation of self that neither the baby nor the baby's audience is willing to support. A recent Twitter posting addresses this concern: "Look: I don't hate babies! I just wish THEY could control the privacy settings on their parents' FB accounts" (BROrococo 2012).

A newborn child already has a digital presence based on hospital and other administrative records (Wood 2006). Facebook pictures and YouTube videos are a public supplement to that presence. While baby photography itself is not new, for some users this display has grown from one photograph in their wallet to hundreds of images on a searchable and archived profile. We may speculate about how these parents would they feel if their own baby photos were so visible. My guess is that they would prefer to keep their infancy out of the public eye. This kind of double standard between one's own exposure and the way they expose others is typical of online identity management (Trottier 2012a). Even loved ones are not exempt from users' tendency to share.

When these children become young adults, their digital presence will shift from their parents' endeavor to their own. Again, we cannot foresee what will happen to this content. Their online presence depends on what happens to the platforms on which their content is held. Sites like Facebook and Flickr may continue to grow in the coming years. They may also decline in popularity, or be sold to another company. Whatever the outcome, the future of these platforms will shape how these children are presented online and in public, as a result of the way they are programmed to retain and display content users might have forgotten. Perhaps more importantly, they will also shape how the child understands online exposure, which in turn will shape their behavior in later stages of their life. If potentially embarrassing moments have been documented and broadcast by their parents, we can only imagine what stigma they may reveal online later on. Another likely development is that these same parents will police their children's online behavior when they are old enough to maintain their own Facebook accounts (Mesch 2006; Marx and Steeves 2010).

## Adolescence and High School

Some older digital media users express gratitude that there was no online service like Facebook to document their adolescence (Jurgenson 2012b). For many teenagers, high school is associated with experimentation and self-discovery, including actions they may later regret. In the case of **sexting**, eight percent of 17-year-olds have sent a sexually suggestive image using their cell phone, and 30 percent have received such content (Lenhart 2009). Those who abstain may be the subject of rumors propagated by their classmates (Ringrose et al. 2012). Falsified stigmas can still cause social harm when peers interpret them as being truthful (cf. Thomas and Thomas 1928). Many young people turn to digital media to maintain their own reputations, but also to either support or damage the reputations of their peers.

Bullying is often framed as a physical ordeal, but it also has a communicative component that can be transferred online (Juvonen and Gross 2008). More than a quarter of adolescents who use mobile phones were harassed on these devices (Lenhart et al. 2010a). In this case, the social media service is the repository for psychological abuse, and mobile phones are the devices that transmit this harm. We may wonder if anonymity—or at least facelessness—amplifies this kind of harassment. Scholars have observed that mediated communication, in comparison to face-to-face exchanges, "insulated teens from the consequences of their actions" (Shariff 2008: 76). These teenagers may know each other, but they do not have to face one other when they circulate stigmatizing details through digital media.

Bullying may leak from high-school hallways onto digital media. Leaks can also flow in the opposite direction, such as when a student's online presence is revealed to his or her peers. In 2009, 14 percent of American teenagers maintained blogs (Lenhart et al. 2010b). These blogs may serve as outlets for personal troubles. However, this otherwise vital act of self-expression can become stigmatizing if discovered by classmates. Users who finished high school before the rise of Facebook may consider themselves lucky for avoiding such risks. However, past stigma may creep back into users' lives when peers document this life stage on the Internet. The online service *Classmates. com* long predates social media, and boasts "over 160,000 digitized high-school yearbooks available for you to view and share photos" (Classmates 2013). Likewise, former classmates may scan analog photographs from yearbooks, and discuss embarrassing anecdotes on platforms like Facebook.

### College, Parties, and Other Regrets

Before spreading to the broader public, Facebook was the exclusive domain of university students. Spring break and study sessions were both coordinated and documented online. Universities no longer monopolize Facebook content, but students remain an over-represented category on this platform. College life is typically framed in terms of experimentation, and many first-year students that I interviewed planned to edit or close their profiles upon graduation (Trottier 2012b). Yet questionable Halloween costumes, binge drinking, and acts of poor judgment are retained online. Consider the highly publicized example of Prince Harry wearing Nazi uniform at a costume party. His status as British royalty means that this incident will not soon fade from public memory. Of course, being a prince also means that he can get away with such incidents. Other users undoubtedly have fewer resources to cope with digital stigma. Stigmatizing photographs might be obscured as users submit more recent content to their Facebook profiles. Yet evidence of past misjudgments and character flaws can remain accessible through Facebook's search function.

Approximately 30 percent of Facebook users have not pursued a college degree (Hampton et al. 2011). Yet these users may encounter similar risks upon entering adulthood. Even had Clementi and Ravi (see Chapter I) not been students, moving away from home for the first time can be emotionally precarious. At this stage, young people may still be negotiating their identities. A new roommate may discover more about a user than the latter would prefer, and may turn to digital media in order to broadcast these details without the other's consent. This exposure may have devastating effects on a user's well-being.

## Romance and Relationships

Relationships can be a milestone in an individual's life. They may also be spoiled by stigma, as well as become a source of stigma in and of themselves. A study commissioned by *Match.com* in 2010 found that one in six recently married couples had met through online dating (Chadwick Martin Bailey 2010). An absence of explicit dating rituals online means that users are learning the "rules and behaviors that minimize 'risky' encounters and can lead to 'successful' online meeting" (Hardey 2008: 1112). Users attempt to establish trust through an optimal amount of self-disclosure whereby embarrassing details are avoided. Would-be suitors construct profiles in a manner that combines self-presentation and stigma management. They deliberately build an online presence that broadcasts positive attributes, all while minimizing the visibility of perceived shortcomings (Toma and Hancock 2010). Age, weight, height, income, and unemployment become stigmatizing in this context, to say nothing of more profound social blemishes.

Online suitors have developed techniques to present themselves in the most flattering manner. This deception is justified by an emerging collective understanding of appropriate signifiers to stretch the truth, and a kind of temporal flexibility where the profile's front stage can refer to a past state or future ideal (Ellison, Hancock, and Toma 2012). Yet these strategies also become a new source of embarrassment. Researchers have considered how users will criticize those who engage in too much strategic self-presentation, notably when they use the so-called "**Myspace angle**" (Sessions 2009). This refers to when a user photographs themselves from a top-down angle, and then crops that photograph in order to obscure stigmatizing features. Self-presentation on dating sites is a strategic compromise between "comprehensively honest and selectively positive self-presentation" (Ellison, Hancock, and Toma 2012: 47). Ellison and her colleagues consider the online profile as a kind of "promise" whereby *"future face-to-face interaction will take place with someone who does not differ fundamentally from the person represented by the profile"* (ibid: 56, emphasis in original). If a user is unable to pass as the self they construct online, others may dismiss them as morally flawed. Identity play is a two-way promise in the context of online dating, and an explicit breach of this promise can be treated as blemish of character. This is a context where users actively seek each other's stigma while concealing their own (Whitty 2008).

In the case of a breakup, a user may decide to share their ex's secrets on social media, especially if they already shared passwords to each other's accounts (Richtel 2012). A scorned ex may also spoil their former partner's reputation by posting compromising pictures of them on a **"revenge" website**. The now-defunct site *isanyoneup.com* exemplified the culture surrounding this process. Not only would users post compromising pictures of former and unrequited partners, but other users would also post comments about the target's physical and moral attributes. The site was eventually shut, in part because of the unintended risk of distributing child pornography (Chen 2012). Revenge sites speak to the social aspect of stigma and shame. Sometimes an individual is personally ashamed of a feature or trait. Yet repulsion from peers may compel someone with an otherwise healthy self-image to be ashamed of their moral and physical attributes.

## Job Applications and Retention

Much like a first date, job applications are typically managed with meticulous care. Applicants are expected to prepare a résumé, which is a summary of their relevant achievements and qualifications. Yet the résumé may be supplemented or even displaced by publicly accessible personal information online. This raises the question of what is actually evaluated in a hiring process. The résumé is meant to display the candidate's qualifications and skills. An employer may be able to discern some kind of stigma, especially of the "given-off" variety. For instance, a two-year gap in a candidate's employment record suggests that they were unemployed, or coping with something more discreditable like substance abuse. A social media presence typically yields more personal information than a résumé, including details users do not want to share with a potential employer. Some social media services are putting these details to use. In 2013 LinkedIn released an algorithm called Recruiter, which recommends individual users to employers on the basis of their profile content (Anders 2013). The analysis this algorithm performs is not transparent, and users are not informed whether they are labeled as employable.

Beyond the scrutiny of a candidate's public presence on sites like Facebook, employers may ask for account passwords in order to access private content (Valdes 2012). The kind of visibility provided by an open profile cannot be overstated. An employer—but most likely a member of the employer's IT staff—can uncover an extensive biography made up of candid photographs and private messages. With a user name and password, they can also search a Facebook user's inbox correspondences, which is a blatant privacy violation. Facebook's staff warns against this practice, noting "if an employer sees on Facebook that someone is a member of a protected group (e.g. over a certain age, etc.) that employer may open themselves up to claims of discrimination if they don't hire that person" (Egan 2012). However, avoiding such exposure involves denying a prospective employer's request for access, which may also harm a candidate's chances of being hired.

## Death and Dying

Coming to terms with death is part of the human condition. Different cultures rely on practices and beliefs to cope with dying, which serve to brace individuals against the initial shock, help them make sense of the loss, and reinforce social ties among the living (Kearl 1989). Death and dying are made meaningful through mass media, and recent scholarship suggests that digital media can be therapeutic for coping with mortality (Wagner, Knaevelsrud, and Maercker 2006). Yet sites like Facebook were initially designed for a living user's immediate context, rather than to mourn that user's passing. Facebook used to removed users' profiles when they died. Following the 2007 Virginia Tech shooting, they began "**memorializing**" this content by transferring the deceased user's online presence to their friends and family (Hortobagyi 2007). Scholars describe memorial pages as an opportunity for users to collectively and publicly mourn the deceased (Forman, Kern, and Gil-Egui 2012).

An individual reputation is a collective product (Solove 2007a), and when an individual passes on, all that remains is what their peers say about them. Typically this would occur in a fixed context, like a funeral home or a wake. In contrast, social media are pervasive and archived. Users can comment on the deceased without concern for their reputation, and these comments can remain online indefinitely. This post-mortem presence can be troubling, as some details are best forgotten when an individual passes on. These details can also have legal consequences, for example, when a memorial page dedicated to a murdered Toronto woman violated a police media ban (CBC 2008).

This chapter considered different stages in a digital media user's life, and how their use of services like Facebook can potentially lead to digital stigma. This cursory overview suggests that digital stigma can be harmful at a formative stage, as it can potentially follow a person beyond that stage and have a lasting impact on their social well-being. Digital stigma can also arise at important junctures in a user's life-course, such as meeting a potential life-partner, or taking up a new job. In recognition that digital media can have a significant presence in users' lives, we may question how users cope with stigma. Chapter V addresses this topic in greater detail.

## DISCUSSION QUESTIONS

1.  Is it fair to claim that various life stages have changed because of online exposure, or is this technological hype? If social life has changed, what kinds of conditions will users born into digital media experience?
2.  When it comes to coping with exposure and digital stigma, is it more challenging to be a so-called digital native, or a so-called digital immigrant?
3.  Will it be possible for users to escape past instances of stigma, or will these have a cumulative effect on their reputations?

# V: The Aftermath of Digital Stigma: Living with a Spoiled Identity

This chapter focuses on the aftermath of digital stigma; that is, how individuals cope with spoiled identities. It considers several prominent examples and highlights their dramaturgical relevance. The previous chapter presented digital stigma as a widespread concern among users, as they may experience it differently depending on their life stage. We may believe that an individual's ability to cope with digital stigma varies according to their life stage, but it is also affected by other factors such as gender, ethnicity, sexual identity, and their access to various forms of capital. In Clementi's case, we can speculate that the lack of a proximate and effective support network, coupled with the perceived severity of the stigma he experienced, made his ordeal insurmountable.

Goffman introduced several concepts that explain how people cope with stigma. First he maintained a distinction between those who are **discredited** and those who are **discreditable** (1963: 14). People who are discredited possess a stigma that is visible to an extent that makes it inescapable. An example of a discrediting stigma is a facial tattoo that denotes the bearer served time in prison. In contrast, being discreditable means that an individual is able to hide their stigma, but the possibility that it may leak into the public is ever-present. Those living with digital stigma may suffer an initial embarrassment, which may then be buried under a continual procession of other personal details. Yet the affordances of digital media render them discreditable, as a search query can retrieve the stigmatizing details. Discreditable users do not always display their stigma, but they face the risk their stigma will resurface.

Goffman also uses terms like the **own** and the **wise** to designate those who possess stigma, and those who are aware of this stigma (ibid.: 31). Those who are wise are not stigmatized, but they are knowledgeable and accepting of a particular stigma. Both own and wise provide support, as the discreditable and discredited can confide in them without fear of further embarrassment or discrimination. Learning how to cope with their stigma is part of a broader **moral career** (ibid.: 45). Coping with contemporary stigma likely entails a different kind of moral career than when Goffman wrote *Stigma*, in part because values and attitudes surrounding stigma are dynamic. For example, homosexuality is no longer diagnosed as a mental disorder (Spitzer 1981), and Americans are more accepting of interracial dating (Wellner 2005). As well, digital media users are not a homogenous population, and we may speculate that their differences will shape their ability to manage stigma. The examples below serve as a cursory overview of how users cope with spoiled identities online. Reflecting on these cases provides insight into how digital media cultures and technological affordances enable digital stigma, but also how biographical differences shape a user's ability to cope.

## Short-term and Long-term Consequences

Immediately after experiencing digital stigma, an individual user may endure social harm. The visibility of their stigma is augmented as a result of their use of digital media, and they may believe that it is inescapable. As Solove remarks: "When shaming occurs online, it ceases to be a temporary mark of disgrace and becomes a lasting inscription of stigma. Permanent shame can be unproductive. It punishes people for longer than necessary and it prevents them from building new lives" (2007a: 96). Consider the 2011 riot in Vancouver. Following the Stanley Cup final between the Vancouver Canucks and the Boston Bruins, hundreds of thousands of people poured into the streets, smashed windows, looted stores, and set fire to civilian and police cars. Participants and spectators used digital cameras and other mobile devices to document the event. Within a few hours, many of these photos were posted on Facebook, and users pooled their efforts to name and shame suspected rioters. Unlike previous riots, participants' visibility was greatly amplified (Schneider and Trottier 2012). These people had to cope with the consequences of their alcohol-induced, mob-mentality actions. They were embroiled in a virtual witch-hunt.

Within a few days, several participants were made visible and stigmatized as a result of social media activity. Camille Cacnio, a local university student, was caught on video looting a clothing store. She was publicly identified as a rioter, a stigma that carried a heavy burden in a city that was looking for a scapegoat. On the Facebook group that identified her, Cacnio became the target of a lot of hateful speech, much of which was both sexist and racially charged. This hate campaign spread elsewhere on the Internet, with an immediate impact on her quality of life. Cacnio's employer fired her, and she attained an online infamy for what may become the most discrediting event in her life (CBC 2011a). On the basis of this short-term impact, we may believe that Cacnio is unable to overcome this shame. Yet Cacnio's long-term outcome is not evident. Perhaps these records will be buried under the billions of pieces of digital content that are uploaded every day. Evidence of her involvement in the riot features prominently among Google's search results. Yet this may change when subsequent riots are documented online. In addition, it is possible that digital media users develop a more forgiving attitude toward those caught in such shameful acts, as new technologies that are quickly domesticated force a reconsideration of social values (Silverstone and Haddon 1996; boyd 2010). Public discourse typically frames rioters as an anonymous gathering of "criminals, anarchists and thugs" (CBC 2011b). Yet now that users are able to identify people who participate in riots, they might balance this stigma against other achievements, such as the university scholarship that Cacino received.

When an individual's reputation is compromised by digital stigma, it is difficult to anticipate the outcome. Consider Ghyslain Raza, also known as the Star Wars Kid. In 2002, Raza recorded a video in which he mimicked a fight scene from *Star Wars* using a golf ball retriever. He filmed this performance with his school's audiovisual equipment. His classmates found and uploaded the video to the Internet, and it spread extensively on peer-to-peer file-sharing networks. His was one of the first instances of high-profile online embarrassment. Raza's performance went public in a way that exemplifies the term "going viral." The initial effects of his exposure were devastating. Raza dropped out of school, and sought psychiatric care after being subjected to so much public ridicule and humiliation. His parents even filed a lawsuit against the students who uploaded the video, citing the extensive toll it had taken on him (Wired 2003). However, after a few years of relative obscurity, Raza made a public comeback. In addition to becoming a lawyer and the president of his hometown's cultural preservation society, he also developed a confidence that suggests a kind of immunity to the previously scathing embarrassment (Nastasi 2010).

We can interpret Raza's recovery from two perspectives. On the one hand, it is possible that digital media culture enabled him to overcome digital stigma. His case was unprecedented, perhaps to a degree that left him no choice but to embrace this overwhelming exposure. Yet perhaps it is the extent of his exposure that makes his case unique. Raza's *Star Wars* antics are considered to be one of the first truly viral videos. Not only did it gain tremendous publicity, but it was also parodied on several television programs. In addition to a psychological toll, Raza experienced a degree of fame that other users will never know. Most people facing digital stigma will not be featured on *Family Guy* and *Arrested Development*, but will instead cope with a damaged reputation and social persecution. Moreover, Raza's ability to recover from his infamy may be attributed to social and economic capital that is also not accorded to all digital media users. After all, Raza could afford the tuition for his law degree, and was invited to participate in a prominent civil society organization.

## How Common is Digital Stigma?

Even if a user is cautious on platforms like Facebook, their peers may upload content that is taken out of context. In my own interviews with social media users, they acknowledge that their vigilance does not prevent unwanted exposure (Trottier 2012a). In particular, photos at parties featuring alcohol were a common source of digital stigma. If such content is so common among a particular group of users, we may speculate that these users could develop a kind of acceptance of party photos and other moments of low-level indiscretion. Yet this culture would likely still persecute those who bear more substantial stigma. In addition, some users will have greater access to resources to manage their online reputation. They may be able to invest more time and money into sanitizing their online reputation. Judging from the rise of services like *Reputation.com*, managing one's online reputation may become a luxury that not all individuals can afford. Moreover, some users will be the target of greater scrutiny and judgment. A person applying for university may not be turned down because of an objectionable party photograph, but the same photograph could harm their career as a public servant. Likewise, an American citizen traveling to Mexico on a holiday may not have to worry about being profiled at the border on the basis of digital stigma. A Mexican citizen crossing in the other direction to take up a job offer may not be as fortunate.

Not all users can cope with digital stigma equally. It would help to consider the notion of the digital divide. This used to be treated as a distinction between those who had access to digital media, and those who lacked access (Wresch 1996). With the increased domestication of personal and mobile computing, coupled with an over 500 percent increase of Internet users worldwide between 2000 and 2011 (Internet-WorldStats 2012), the division between haves and have-nots seems to have receded, or is at least no longer determined by access. Subsequent research considers that a contemporary divide is based on skill (van Deursen and van Dijk 2011), cultural differences (Harambam, Aupers, and Houtman 2012) and personal identity (Goode 2010). Even if all individuals had equal access to digital media, discrepancies on the basis of media literacy as well as other resources such as time and money are likely to shape their ability to manage digital stigma. Inequality as manifest online will surely continue to be a topic of discussion, but it remains clear that the interaction of all the above factors means that some users will be more prepared to cope with this visibility than others. Furthermore, individuals who are not online, whether by choice or due to a lack of capital, may increasingly experience discrimination as a result of their abstention. For example, many landlords in New York City are reluctant to rent apartments to young people whom they cannot locate on Facebook (Morozov 2013). Thus, non-users may experience greater difficulty securing shelter because they are not visible online.

Users may speculate whether party photos and other mundane kinds of stigma will spoil their reputation. It seems unreasonable that party photos could cause social harm, considering that such photographs are common features of North American digital media culture (Hearn 2008). However, professional roles rely on a social barrier separating the professional from the personal (Gutheil and Gabbard 1993). Digital media culture contributes to the dissolution of that barrier. Another concern is that treating stigma as ubiquitous contributes to a belief that all stigmas are treated equally. Even if all users have something to hide, they do not face the same consequences. An embarrassing picture from a night of partying is not the same as a lifelong bowel disorder, or a prison record. Digital media might augment the discovery of these personal details, but that does not mean that the aftermath is the same for all discoveries.

## Reconsidering Life in the Public Eye

Digital media are often treated as a kind of public, as users turn to these services in order to interact with others. From this perspective, we may consider them as a 21st-century version of the agora, where citizens gather to exchange ideas (Papacharissi 2002). However, this is only one of many purposes that digital media serve. The problem with convergence technologies like Facebook is that their affordances are disparate. People use Facebook for public broadcasts, but also for more intimate conversations. Because it is not used exclusively as a kind of digital megaphone, it seems reasonable that users should expect some degree of privacy. Here, we may treat privacy as synonymous with Goffman's back stage (see Chapter 1). It is the location where users can suspend their performances and cope with stigmatizing attributes. In principle, privacy settings on digital media offer a kind of protection from public exposure. Yet in practice they frequently fail to protect users' personal information (boyd 2008a). For example, friends located within a user's private inner-circle can leak information to a broader public. This can happen accidentally when they comment on a private status update, and re-broadcast it to their own personal network. Or they may intentionally leak it. Furthermore, digital media platforms often undergo revisions, exposing users' private content in the process (Stutzman, Gross, and Acquisiti 2012). Users are aware of these concerns, and develop tactics to both manage and make sense of privacy on these platforms (boyd 2011). When discussing her own exposure on Facebook, a 20-something user I interviewed referred to it as a "completely public expression of private and personal matters" (Trottier 2012a: 326). Framed thusly, her use of digital media results in an augmented exposure of her personal matters.

Perhaps it is not possible to identify a back stage on digital media. Maybe users can only access a back stage when they log off Facebook. Or perhaps they need to dispense with the notion of the back stage. Many scholars have argued that a binary (that is, front stage/back stage) understanding of privacy is limited. Individuals do not practice confidentiality in absolute terms; rather, privacy is **contextual** (Nissenbaum 2009). Individuals present different aspects of themselves in different settings. A user may be comfortable sharing some information with their friends, other information to their employer, and still other information to their therapist. Yet they would not want these three groups to exchange these details with each other. This exchange is precisely the social problem caused by converging contexts on digital and social media.

The conventional functioning of digital devices and platforms relies on user visibility. As a result, their privacy may be compromised. Is it fair to say that they are living in a fully transparent, post-privacy world? We may consider reality television programs as indicative of a post-privacy and post-shame culture. In particular, makeover reality programs such as *What Not to Wear* enroll seemingly ordinary individuals to undergo an invasive and often humiliating evaluation of their private lives. While the tone of these shows is rehabilitative, viewers are invited to enjoy the humiliation that participants experience (Dovey 2000). An immediate reaction may be to dismiss the quality and relevance of these programs. Yet this assessment overlooks the fact that embarrassment is normalized on mass and social media (Van Zoonen 2001). Perhaps we are witnessing an emerging post-shame culture, where digital media users are immune to formerly stigmatizing attributes. Or perhaps participants are simply willing to embarrass themselves in exchange for the fame that is contained within infamy.

Regardless of digital media culture, most users likely do not upload personal details in order to attain viral infamy. How can they prevent this outcome? A bit of self-care is important, and many Facebook users are acutely aware of the informal protocols that govern self-presentation online. When it comes to hiding a stigmatizing feature, they may heighten their privacy settings, purge unprofessional content from their profile, or construct a sanitized alternate profile (Trottier 2012a). Yet the most effective tactic to manage embarrassing online content is simply not to upload it. Self-censorship may be an effective tactic, but one's peers can still put a user at risk. By virtue of being connected to friends on social networks, they have the ability to speak on a users' behalf, for instance, by posting a photograph of them with an illicit substance. Friends who had no intention of harming one another can do so through negligent use of social media. Therefore, self-care should be supplemented by care for the other (Lyon 2007), notably by exercising caution about how a user's actions online reflect on their peers. Users ought to consider how peers want to appear in specific contexts, and what details they might wish to remain private.

## DISCUSSION QUESTIONS

1. Stigma is a potential concern for digital media users. Yet online businesses allow people to repair their reputation. Are we witnessing a growing disparity between those who can afford to manage their reputations online, and those who are at the mercy of digital media culture?

2. Some types of embarrassing content like party photos are common, and many users may be presented online in a compromised state. Will this content continue to harm users' professional reputations, or will users become immune to this effect?

3. To what extent is the rise of embarrassing online content shaped by a media culture that privileges easy laughs at the expense of other people and their reputations?

# VI: Conclusion: What's Next?
# New Technologies, New Opportunities
# for Digital Stigma

~~~⌒~~~

This book concludes with an overview of digital stigma based on the previous chapters. It then presents some counterpoints to our understanding of this social problem. Finally, it considers how new technologies can contribute to a dramaturgical understanding of online reputations. This includes the rise of social advertising, geolocational services, and maintaining a long-term presence on social media. Based on our understanding of digital stigma, we may extrapolate new challenges and risks to users' reputations.

In order to understand how identities can be spoiled through digital media, we first considered 20th-century sociologist Erving Goffman. His work on micro-level interactions provides a dramaturgical approach to social life, whereby individuals treat their social environment as a stage. Front-stage performances involve concealing personal details in order to avoid social embarrassment. Digital media's growing popularity has complicated users' performances. Users may not fully understand the stage upon which they perform, and compromising details may be leaked to the public. Not only do users need to develop new strategies to avoid stigma, but they also need to consider the relation between technologies and social problems.

Chapter 2 focused on the emergence of contemporary digital media culture. We began by looking at identity management as it was conceived in the early days of the Internet. A particular set of values in the late 20th century celebrated a flexible form of self-presentation. Early online communities privileged the free exchange of ideas, as well as a less totalizing attitude toward identity. Yet the Internet's popularity contributed to a shift in how users interacted online. Instead of turning to confidential spaces to address a specific issue, many users now rely on cross-contextual and highly visible platforms. Facebook is an exemplar of Web 2.0 services that are designed to distribute user-generated content, especially personal information. This shift contributed to the kinds of stigma and social embarrassment that trouble many users in the 21st century.

Digital stigma forces a reconsideration of the social impact of technologies in the domestic realm. Chapter 3 provided an overview of social scientific understandings of technologies. A technological deterministic approach considers the social and cultural effects of introducing a new device or software. Yet this approach overlooks the fact that these technologies do not exist in a social vacuum. This issue is remedied by a social constructionist approach. Scholarship that focuses on the social construction of digital media considers the intentions and ideologies of those who produce and market services like Facebook, but also journalists and scholars who report about them as well as the hundreds of millions of users who contribute to their domestication. However, the technologies that social actors construct also influence those social actors. A mutual shaping approach presents a symbiotic relationship between technologies and society. Individuals inscribe specific values into the technologies they use, which in turn determine what they are capable of doing with them. Most digital media are designed for self-expression, and users may feel compelled to disclose personal information. Further, the more users are acclimatized to these technologies, the more influence they exert over users' lives, especially when they creep into other social contexts.

Users' ability to cope with digital stigma depends on their social circumstances. Chapter 4 considers digital stigma at several stages of an individual's life course. Many children have an extensive online presence as a result of their parents' activity on sites like Facebook. In high school, bullying, rumors, and angst may be documented and distributed across digital media. As young adults, evidence of debauchery and experimentation may linger because of tagged photographs. These may be assessed as blemishes of character, and users may be held accountable to this content. Relationships risk being compromised by personal details found online. Even in death, users are not immune to stigma. In fact, their reputations are passed on to their peers. This overview suggests that digital stigma is not bound to any single life stage. Rather, it is a heterogeneous problem shaped by a user's social context.

Digital media's saturation in many users' lives means that stigma is a relevant concern in the 21st century. Chapter 5 focused on examples of digital stigma to consider how these individuals cope with this problem. Although digital stigma can be harmful in the short term, some individuals appear to recover from their online infamy. We may speculate that exposure to so much stigmatizing content online contributes to a more forgiving digital media culture. Alternatively, it is possible that only a few media-friendly, stigma-based celebrities are able to flourish under so much digital scrutiny, while other users struggle with the unwanted exposure of their personal details.

This book has argued that digital media culture contributes to stigma in the 21st century. Yet we may question whether digital stigma is a pervasive and harmful social problem. Some counter-arguments may be helpful. Digital stigma is not a homogenous social problem: not everyone is online, not everyone who is online is vulnerable, and those who cope with stigma do not cope with it to the same degree. Yet even taking digital media at face value raises issues that are considered below.

## Enough with the Internet Shame!

In response to the ubiquity of online exposure, some may argue that users should not be preoccupied with impression management, and should instead accept the idea of living online. Moreover, users should not consider all personal information as stigmatizing, nor should they treat every stigma as a source of personal shame. We may question the extent to which commercial interests fuel users' sense of stigma. In particular, advertisements and other commercial media present arbitrary standards to viewers, and attempt to invoke shame among viewers if they fail to meet these standards (Wykes and Gunter 2005). Consider the combination of reality television and the commercials that sponsor them. Reality television commodifies the participant's private realm in order to highlight their physical and emotional shortcomings (Deery 2004). Such programming is followed by commercials for products that allegedly resolve these shortcomings. Users should not let a shame-based media culture hinder their online presence. Seemingly anything can be framed as a source of shame, including underarm sweat, a messy closet, and the previous generation of mobile phones. We may hope that users refute these messages. Yet even if users are comfortable with their online presence, they still have to contend with assessments made by other social actors, including romantic partners and employers.

## Full-on Privacy is Problematic

The digital world is often framed as a new kind of public (Papacharissi 2002), and privacy concerns should be balanced in recognition of this function. Privacy, or the right to be let alone (Warren and Brandeis 1890), is an inalienable right. And users are certainly entitled to have embarrassing details withheld from online platforms. Yet framing every interaction on digital media as a potential privacy risk is problematic. On an individual level, users risk overlooking the benefits of online communication. As seen in Chapter II, one of the guiding visions of the early web was as a space for self-expression and self-actualization. Exposure on digital media is closely linked to this vision. After all, users embrace online visibility for empowerment (Koskela 2006) and control (White 2003). They may choose to actively participate in their exposure (Albrechtslund 2008). However, willful exposure may still result in unanticipated consequences, such as surveillance creep and profiling.

On a broader scale, communities benefit from public spaces where individuals can engage socially, culturally, and politically with others. The public sphere is a vital component of civil society (Habermas 1989). Yet during the 20th century, parks and public squares have been privatized, public media are succumbing to commercial pressure, and private shopping centers are default locations for public gatherings. As a result, online spaces are all the more crucial for civic engagement, especially because their potential for social good is not embedded in digital media, but rather in user adoption of these media (Papacharissi 2002). Focusing exclusively on instances where they compromise users' reputations undermines their potential.

## Mistaking a Social Problem for an Individual Concern

If digital stigma is a social problem, it should be met with a sense of social responsibility. In Chapter V, I argued that users should be concerned with how they impact their peers' reputation as much as how their peers impact them. Both vulnerabilities speak to the inherently collective nature of a problem that is too often framed as an individual concern. The study of social problems should be rooted in the perspective that individual troubles are in fact the product of particular social conditions, and that these conditions could be otherwise. Individual stigmas are a collective problem: they are the product of shared cultural values as well as digital media that can be used to distribute stigmatizing content. Rather than merely prescribing individual users to take responsibility for their online selves (Whitson and Haggerty 2008), privacy advocates and other public figures should petition for safer and more reliable communication online (Bennett 2008).

## Anticipating New Technologies

The platforms and devices described in this book are supplemented by emerging technologies. While users are coming to terms with the consequences of their presence on Facebook, these new technologies may complicate those consequences. To be clear, new technologies do not inherently shape the social world. Rather, their impact is based on how users adopt them, and how they are made meaningful within a broader digital media culture. Below we will consider how these emerging technologies may possibly shape how users cope with online stigma.

In the 21st century market researchers have sought to revise broadcast advertising. In addition to classifying market segments based on postal codes and spending habits (Burrows and Gane 2006), they use digital media to target individuals with finely tuned **social advertisements**. Digital media platforms are typically saturated with ads such that routine activities like checking one's email or consulting a weather forecast can generate commercial messages. Furthermore, online platforms collect details about users such as their hardware and software, but also more personal information culled from emails, chats, and messages. Taken together, this information builds a profile that determines the kinds of ads users will receive. If they recently searched prospective law schools on Google, they may encounter ads about the LSAT exams. If they emailed a close friend about marital woes, they may receive ads for a counselor, or an infidelity-themed dating service. These systems are a kind of classification system based on personal and often stigmatizing information. Consider the potential embarrassment if these ads—or the online profile that determines these ads—became public knowledge. Users might not even remember what they searched to warrant ads for weight loss or penile enhancement pills. A user's multi-contextual online presence is reduced to a potentially stigmatizing category. The extent to which targeted ads collect user details is a clear privacy concern (Evans 2009), most notably because seemingly private details can leak into the public domain. And the risk of such leaks will likely increase if online advertising becomes more pervasive. Of course, this risk depends on how users cope with this new technology, as their reception of social advertising can influence its impact on how they are represented.

The Internet used to be framed as a separate location from the "real" world, but contemporary digital media culture challenges the online/offline distinction. The arrival of **geolocation** services further complicates this distinction. Nearly every popular social media allows users to disclose their spatial location. On Facebook, users can "check in" at their favorite restaurant, but other content like status updates and images can also be identified by location. A user may willfully provide this information, but it is also a default feature, such that users can unknowingly disclose their trajectory over a period of time. Likewise, photos taken with an iPhone or other devices retain their location by default as a form of metadata. These services drew controversy when they were introduced. Privacy critics highlighted their potential for social harm, noting "locational privacy is being challenged in ways that affect individual consumer and constitutional protections" (EPIC 2012). Many users considered this technology to be vaguely creepy, but today's "creepy" could be tomorrow's "cool" (Robbins 2012).

Geolocation poses a possible social risk in the long run. Users may be comfortable sharing their location in a specific point in time, with a specific group of people. This information lingers online, and can be employed for secondary purposes that we have not anticipated (cf. Lyon 2007). For instance, the entirety of a user's "check-ins" to their local pub can present that user as a borderline alcoholic. Yet if it also reveals that they walk several miles to "check in" at the pub, perhaps this will offer a more balanced composite image of harm and health. Of course, cultural values surrounding locational privacy will be shaped by the domestication of these services. Location-based digital stigma may recede as a result of users' continued exposure to such services.

The next technology is not new per se, but an emerging condition of existing media. Even if users abstain from new technologies that gather personal information, they may continue to use the ones they already know. If so, they may discover how a prolonged exposure to these technologies will affect their reputations. **Long-term data collection** is a growing concern. Users engage with services like Facebook on a short-term basis. They communicate with others, or simply express themselves, with an immediate context in mind (Davis 2010). Yet prolonged use of social media contributes to a kind of personal repository that exceeds any particular context. How will a Facebook profile be assessed if it contains 20 years' worth of personal data? It is reasonable to assume that some broader patterns will emerge (cf. Andrejevic 2013). Any single status update may be harmless, but when processed in aggregate they may reveal troubling details about users' dispositions. Imagine a job interview in 2025 where employers rely on software to scrutinize two decades' worth of tweets and status updates (much of which might be publicly accessible), and label candidates with any number of personality and conduct disorders. Indeed, this kind of classification is an immediate possibility (Walker 2012). Privacy advocates are concerned that "those who crunch Big Data with algorithms might draw the wrong conclusions about who someone is, how she might behave in the future, and how to apply the correlations that will emerge in the data analysis" (Anderson and Raine 2012). Placing greater confidence in a person's data, and less in the actual person, is a possible concern with long-term data.

### Conclusion: What if We Could Delete our Presence?

Based on the above risks, users might demand greater control over the information they upload. Imagine if users could exercise the "right to be forgotten" online (Rosen 2012). The final technology addressed in this chapter is framed as a potential remedy to digital stigma. Legal scholar Viktor Mayer-Schonberger (2009) has proposed that personal information online could have an expiry date. If this were the case, a user could specify when a photograph or tweet would no longer be accessible. At that point, the content would be removed from the Internet. With a deletion protocol, users could upload potentially stigmatizing content, knowing that it would cease to exist by the time they applied for a job. This may be regarded as an elegant solution to digital stigma. Yet it also raises logistical concerns. For instance, one user may upload a photograph that features a romantic partner. The user may set an expiry date, but their partner may have a conflicting request. Furthermore, a third party may print a physical copy of that image and circulate it long past its expiry date. Putting this type of deletion technology into practice would complicate online identity management. Just as digital media do not directly cause digital stigma, perhaps it is unreasonable to expect a technological fix to this problem.

### DISCUSSION QUESTIONS

1. Digital media can contribute to stigma, and new devices may pose a risk for similar harm. Is it possible to anticipate and prevent such harm before these technologies are released to the public?
2. Some users have been on Facebook for as long as it has been available. In addition, they have maintained weblogs and profiles on other sites, culminating in a long-term presence online. What effect might such a presence have on their reputations?
3. Would you use a social media site that offered the possibility to set an expiry date on information you uploaded? What kinds of problems do you anticipate if this became the new default for sharing online?

# References

Abbate, Janet. 1999. *Inventing the Internet.* Cambridge, MA: MIT Press.

Albrechtslund, Anders. 2008. "Online social networking as participatory surveillance." *First Monday* *13*(3). Accessed online at http://firstmonday.org/htbin/cgiwrap/bin/ojs/index.php/fm/article/view/2142/1949

Alexa. 2012. "The top 500 sites on the web." Accessed online at http://www.alexa.com/topsites

Anders, George. 2013. "Who should you hire? LinkedIn says: Try our algorithm." *Forbes.* Retrieved April 10, 2013 (http://www.forbes.com/sites/georgeanders/2013/04/10/who-should-you-hire-linkedin-says-try-our-algorithm)

Anderson, Janna and Lee Raine. 2012. "Big data: Experts say new forms of information analysis will help people be more nimble and adaptive, but worry over humans' capacity to understand and use these new tools well." Pew Internet & American Life Project. Retrieved July 20, 2012 (http://pewinternet.org/~/media//Files/Reports/2012/PIP_Future_of_Internet_2012_Big_Data.pdf)

Andrejevic, Mark. 2007. *iSpy: Surveillance and power in the interactive era.* Lawrence, KS: University Press of Kansas.

——— 2013. *Infoglut: How too much information is changing the way we think and know.* New York: Routledge.

Arthur, Charles. 2012. "Employers warned against demanding Facebook details from staff: ICO says it would have 'very serious concerns' if UK employers asked employees for Facebook login and password details." The *Guardian.* Retrieved March 26, 2012 (www.guardian.co.uk/technology/2012/mar/26/employers-warned-facebook-login-details/print)

Barbrook, Richard. 2000. "Cyber-communism: How the Americans are superseding capitalism in cyberspace." *Science as Culture 9*(1): 5–40.

BBC. 2010. "Over 5 billion mobile phone connections worldwide." *BBC News.* July 9, 2010. Accessed online at http://www.bbc.co.uk/news/10569081

Beck, Ulrich. 1992. *Risk society: Toward a new modernity.* London: Sage.

Beer, David and Roger Burrows. 2007. "Sociology and, of and in Web 2.0: Some initial considerations." *Sociological Research Online 12*(5). Accessed online at http://www.socresonline.org.uk/12/5/17.html

Beevolve. 2012. "An exhaustive study of Twitter users across the world." Retrieved October 10, 2012 (http://www.beevolve.com/twitter-statistics)

Bennett, Colin. 2008. *The privacy advocates: Resisting the spread of surveillance.* Cambridge, MA: MIT Press.

Berger, Peter L. and Thomas Luckmann. 1966. *The social construction of reality*. New York: Anchor Books.

Berners-Lee, Tim. 1995. "Hypertext and our collective destiny. " October 12, 1995. Accessed online at http://www.w3.org/Talks/9510_Bush/Talk.html

Bird, S. Elizabeth. 2009. "The future of journalism in the digital environment." *Journalism 10*(3): 293–95.

Boczkowski, Pablo. 2004. "The mutual shaping of technology and society in videotex newspapers: Beyond the diffusion and social shaping perspectives." *The Information Society: An International Journal 20*(4): 255–67.

Boesel, Whtiney Erin. 2012. "Possibility vs. potentiality: A case study in documentary consciousness." *Cyborgology*. July 26, 2012. Accessed online at  http://thesocietypages.org/cyborgology/2012/07/26/possibility-vs-potentiality-a-case-study-in-documentary-consciousness/

Bowker, Geoff and Susan Leigh Star. 1999. *Sorting things out: Classification and its consequences*. Cambridge, MA: MIT Press.

boyd, danah. 2008a. "Facebook's privacy trainwreck: Exposure, invasion, and social convergence." *Convergence: The International Journal of Research into New Media Technologies 14*(1): 13–20.

——— 2008b. "Why youth (heart) social network sites: The role of networked publics in teenage social life." Pp. 119–42 in *Youth, Identity, and Digital Media*, ed. David Buckingham. The John D. and Catherine T. MacArthur Foundation Series on Digital Media and Learning. Cambridge, MA: MIT Press. Accessed online at http://www.ec.tuwien.ac.at/~dieter/teaching/GmA/Boyd2008.pdf

——— 2010. "Social network sites as networked publics: Affordances, dynamics, and implications." Pp. 39–58 in *Networked self: Identity, community, and culture on social network sites*, ed. Zizi Papacharissi. New York: Routledge.

——— 2011. "Dear voyeur, meet flâneur ... sincerely, social media." *Surveillance & Society 8*(4): 505–507.

boyd, danah and Nicole Ellison. 2007. "Social network sites: Definition, history, and scholarship." *Journal of Computer-Mediated Communication 13*(1), Article 11. Accessed online at http://jcmc.indiana.edu/vol13/issue1/boyd.ellison.html

BROrococo. 2012. Accessed online at http://twitter.com/BROrococo/status/245576959361429504

Burrows, Roger and Nick Gane. 2006. "Geo-demographics, software and class." *Sociology 40*(5): 793–812.

Cartoonbank. 2011. "On the Internet, nobody knows  you're a dog." Accessed online at http://www.cartoonbank.com/invt/106197

CBC. 2008. "Facebook phenomenon latest legal obstacle, say critics." *CBC News*. January 4, 2008. Accessed online at http://www.cbc.ca/news/canada/toronto/story/2008/ 01/04/rengel-facebook.html

——— 2011a. "Alleged riot looter fired from job." *CBC News*. June 22, 2011. Accessed online at http://www.cbc.ca/news/canada/british-columbia/story/2011/06/22/bc-rioter-fired.html

——— 2011b. "Vancouver police shift blame for riot." *CBC News*. June 20, 2011. Accessed online at http://www.cbc.ca/news/canada/british-columbia/story/2011/06/20/bc-vancouver-police-riot.html

Chadwick, Martin Bailey. 2010. Match.com and Chadwick Martin Bailey 2009–2010 Studies: Recent Trends: Online Dating. Accessed online at http://cp.match.com/cppp/media/CMB_Study.pdf

Chakrabortty, Aditya. 2010. "Facebook, Google and Twitter: Custodians of our most intimate secrets. We've handed our personal database to Internet companies with hardly any questions asked." The Guardian. May 25, 2010. Accessed online at http://www.guardian.co.uk/commentisfree/2010/may/25/personal-secrets-to-internet-companies

Chen, Adrian. 2012. "Internet's sleaziest pornographer calls it quits: 'I'm done with looking at little kids naked all day.'" Gawker.com. Retrieved April 19, 2012 (http://gawker.com/5903486/internets-sleaziest-pornographer-calls-it-quits-im-done-with-looking-at-little-kids-naked-all-day)

Cheong, Pauline H., Jessie P. H. Poon, Shirlena Huang, and Irene Casas. 2009. "The Internet highway and religious communities: Mapping and contesting spaces in religion-online." The Information Society 25(5): 291–302.

Classmates. 2013. "About us." Classmates.com. Accessed online at http://www.classmates.com/about

Cooley, Charles H. 1922. Human nature and the social order. New York: Scribner's.

Dandeker, Christopher. 1990. Surveillance, power and modernity. Cambridge: Polity Press.

Davis, Jenny. 2010. "Architecture of the personal interactive homepage: Constructing the self through Myspace." New Media & Society 12(7): 1103–19.

Deery, June. 2004. "Reality TV as advertisement." Popular Communication: The International Journal of Media and Culture 2(1): 1–20.

Donath, Judith. 1999. "Identity and deception in the virtual community." Pp. 29–59 in Communities in Cyberspace, ed. Marc Smith and Peter Kollock. New York: Routledge.

Dovey, Jon. 2000. Freakshow: First person media and factual television. London: Pluto Press.

Egan, Erin. 2012. "Protecting your passwords and your privacy." Facebook Privacy. Retrieved March 23, 2012 (https://www.facebook.com/note.php?note_id=326598317390057)

Ellison, Nicole, Charles Steinfield, and Cliff Lampe. 2007. "The benefits of Facebook 'friends': Social capital and college students' use of online social network sites." Journal of ComputerMediated Communication 12(4). Accessed online at http://jcmc.indiana.edu/vol12/issue4/ellison.html

Ellison, Nicole, Jeffrey Hancock, and Catalina Toma. 2012. "Profile as promise: A framework for conceptualizing veracity in online dating self-presentations." New Media & Society 14(1): 45–62.

EPIC. 2012. "Locational privacy." Accessed online at http://epic.org/privacy/location_privacy/default.html

Evans, David. 2009. "The online advertising industry: Economics, evolution, and privacy." Journal of Economic Perspectives 23(3): 37–60.

Evans, Rhonda. 2001. "Examining the informal sanctioning of deviance in a chat room culture." Deviant Behavior 22(3): 195–210.

Facebook. 2013. "Key facts." Accessed online at http://newsroom.fb.com/Key-Facts

Farrell, Hilary. 2012. "Facebook, click fraud, and the deceptive digital advertising landscape." Forbes. Retrieved August 15, 2012 (http://www.forbes.com/sites/benzingainsights/2012/08/15/facebook-click-fraud-and-the-deceptive-digital-advertising-landscape)

Faulkner, Wendy. 2001. "The technology question in feminism: A view from feminist technology studies." Women's Studies International Forum 24(1): 79–95.

FBInfo. 2012. "About Facebook." Accessed online at http://www.facebook.com/facebook/info

Fonio, Chiara, Fabio Giglietto, Romeo Pruno, Luca Rossi, and Stefano Pedriol. 2007. "Eyes on you: Analyzing user-generated content for social science." Paper delivered at the Toward a Social Science of Web 2.0 conference, 5–6 September. York, UK.

Forman, Abbe, Rebecca Kern, and Gisela Gil-Egui. 2012. "Death and mourning as sources of community participation in online social networks: R.I.P. pages in Facebook." *First Monday* 17(9). Accessed online at http://firstmonday.org/htbin/cgiwrap/bin/ojs/index.php/fm/article/view/3935/3288

Fuchs, Christian. 2011. "Web 2.0, prosumption, and surveillance." *Surveillance & Society* 8(3): 288–309.

Galagher, Jolene, Lee Sproull, and Sara Kiesler. 1998. "Legitimacy, authority, and community in electronic support groups." *Written Communication* 15(4): 493–530.

Gandy, Oscar. 1993. *The panoptic sort: A political economy of personal information.* Boulder, CO: Westview Press.

——— 2009. *Coming to terms with chance: Engaging rational discrimination and cumulative disadvantage.* Farnham, UK: Ashgate.

Gearfuse. 2009. "Brother gets sweet, sweet revenge on sister by posting hook-up list on Facebook." Gearfuse.com. Retrieved December 22, 2009 (http://www.gearfuse.com/brother-gets-sweet-sweet-revenge-on-sister-by-posting-hook-up-list-on-facebook)

Giddens, Anthony. 1984. *The constitution of society: Outline of the theory of structuration.* Berkeley, CA: University of California Press.

Goffman, Erving. 1952. "On cooling the mark out: Some aspects of adaptation to failure." *Psychiatry* 15(4): 451–63.

——— 1959. *The presentation of self in everyday life.* New York: Anchor Books.

——— 1961. *Asylums: Essays on the social situation of mental patients and other inmates.* New York: Anchor Books.

——— 1963. *Stigma: Notes on the management of spoiled identity.* New York: Simon and Schuster.

——— 1967. *Interaction ritual: Essays in face-to-face behavior.* Chicago, IL: Aldine.

Goode, Joanna. 2010. "The digital identity divide: How technology knowledge impacts college students." *New Media & Society* 12(3): 497–513.

Google. 2001. "Google acquires Usenet discussion service and significant assets from Deja.com." Accessed onine at http://www.google.com/press/pressrel/pressrelease48.html

Gutheil, Thomas G. and Glen O. Gabbard. 1993. "The concept of boundaries in clinical practice: Theoretical and risk management decisions." *American Journal of Psychiatry* 150(2): 188–96.

Habermas, Jurgen. 1989. *The structural transformation of the public sphere: An inquiry into a category of bourgeois society.* Cambridge, MA: MIT Press.

Hampton, Keith, Lauren Sessions Goulet, Lee Raine, and Kristen Purcell. 2011. "Social networking sites and our lives: How people's trust, personal relationships, and civic and political involvement are connected to their use of social networking sites and other technologies." Pew Research Center's Internet and American Life Project. Accessed online at http://www.pewinternet.org/Reports/2011/Technology-and-social-networks.aspx

Harambam, Jaron, Stef Aupers, and Dick Houtman. 2012. "The contentious gap." *Information, Communication and Society.* Accessed online at http://www.tandfonline.com/doi/abs/10.1080/1369118X.2012.687006

Hardey, Mariann. 2008. "The formation of social rules for digital interactions." *Information, Communication and Society 11*(8): 1111–31.

Hauben, Michael and Ronda Hauben. 1997. "Netizens: On the history and impact of Usenet and the Internet." Los Alamitos, CA: IEEE Computer Society Press. Accessed online at http://www.columbia.edu/~hauben/netbook

Hearn, Alison. 2008. "'Meat, mask, burden': Probing the contours of the branded 'self.'" *Journal of Consumer Culture 8*(2): 197–217.

Hirsch, Adam. 2008. "CNN heavily promoting Twitter on air, making big moves in social media." Mashable. Retrieved September 4, 2008 (http://mashable.com/2008/09/04/cnn-twitter)

Hortobagyi, Monica. 2007. "Slain students' pages to stay on Facebook." *USAToday*. Retrieved May 9, 2007 (http://www.usatoday.com/tech/webguide/internetlife/2007-05-08-facebook-vatech_N.htm)

InternetWorldStats. 2012. "Internet users in the world." Accessed online at http://www.internetworldstats.com/stats.htm

Jernigan, Carter and Behram Mistree. 2009. "Gaydar: Facebook friendships expose sexual orientation." *First Monday 14*(10). Accessed online at http://firstmonday.org/htbin/cgiwrap/bin/ojs/index.php/fm/article/view/2611/2302

Johnson, Bobbie. 2010. "Privacy no longer a social norm, says Facebook founder." The *Guardian*. January 11, 2010. Accessed online at http://www.guardian.co.uk/technology/2010/jan/11/facebook-privacy

Jones, Chris and Binhui Shao. 2011. *The net generation and digital natives: Implications for higher education*. York, UK: Higher Education Academy.

Jurgenson, Nathan. 2012a. "The IRL fetish." *The New Inquiry*. Retrieved June 28, 2012a (http://thenewinquiry.com/essays/the-irl-fetish)

———— 2012b. "'Glad I didn't have Facebook in high-school!'" *Cyborgology*. Retrieved November 26, 2012 (http://thesocietypages.org/cyborgology/2012/11/26/glad-i-didnt-have-facebook-in-high-school)

Juvonen, Jaana and Elisheva Gross. 2008. "Extending the school grounds? Bullying experiences in cyberspace." *Journal of School Health 78*(9): 496–505.

Kearl, Michael. 1989. *Endings: A sociology of death and dying*. Oxford: Oxford University Press.

Kennedy, Helen. 2006. "Beyond anonymity, or future directions for internet identity research." *New Media and Society 8*(6): 859–76.

Koskela, H. 2006. "'The other side of surveillance:' Webcams, power and agency." Pp. 163–81 in *Theorizing surveillance: The panopticon and beyond*, ed. David Lyon. Cullompton, UK: Willan Publishing.

Leigh Star, Susan. 1999. "The ethnography of infrastructure." *American Behavioral Scientist 43*(3): 377–91.

Lenhart, Amanda. 2009. "Teens and sexting: How and why minor teens are sending sexually suggestive nude or nearly nude images via text messaging." *Pew Internet and American Life Project*. Retrieved December 15, 2009 (http://www.pewinternet.org/~/media//Files/Reports/2009/PIP_Teens_and_Sexting.pdf)

Lenhart, Amanda, Rich Ling, Scott Campbell, and Kirsten Purcell. 2010a. "Teens and mobile phones: Text messaging explodes as teens embrace it as the centerpiece of their communication strategies with friends." *Pew Internet and American Life Project*. Retrieved April 20, 2010 (http://pewinternet.org/~/media//Files/Reports/2010/PIP-Teens-and-Mobile-2010-with-topline.pdf)

Lenhart, Amanda, Kristen Purcell, Aaron Smith, and Kathryn Zickuhr. 2010b. "Social media & mobile Internet use among teens and young adults." Pew Internet & American Life Project. Retrieved February 3, 2010 (http://www.pewinternet.org/~/media//Files/Reports/2010/PIP_Social_Media_and_Young_Adults_Report_Final_with_toplines.pdf)

Lyon, David. 2001. *Surveillance society: Monitoring everyday life*. Buckingham: Open University Press.

———— 2007. *Surveillance studies: An overview*. Cambridge: Polity Press.

McLaughlin, Caitlin and Jessica Vitak. 2012. "Norm evolution and violation on Facebook." *New Media and Society 14*(2): 299–315.

Madden, Mary. 2010. "Older adults and social media: Social networking use among those ages 50 and older nearly doubled over the past year." Pew Internet and American Life Project. Accessed online at http://pewinternet.org/Reports/2010/Older-Adults-and-Social-Media.aspx

Martin, Michèle. 1991. *"Hello, Central?": Gender, technology, and culture in the formation of telephone systems*. Montreal: McGill-Queen's Press.

Marx, Gary T. and Valerie Steeves. 2010. "From the beginning: Children as subjects and agents of surveillance." *Surveillance and Society 7*(3/4): 192–230.

Mayer-Schonberger, Viktor. 2009. *Delete: The virtue of forgetting in the digital age*. Princeton, NJ: Princeton University Press.

Mead, George Herbert. 1934. *Mind, self and society*. Chicago, IL: University of Chicago Press.

Mesch, Gustavo. 2006. "Family characteristics and intergenerational conflicts over the Internet." *Information, Communication and Society 9*(4): 473–95.

Meyrowitz, Joshua. 1990. "Redefining the situation: Extending dramaturgy into a theory of social change and media effects". Pp. 65–97 in *Beyond Goffman: Studies on communication, institution, and social interaction*, ed. Stephen Riggins. New York: Mouton de Gruyter.

Microsoft. 2012. "Online predators: Help minimize the risk." Accessed online at http://www.microsoft.com/security/family-safety/predators.aspx

Morozov, Evgeny. 2013. "The folly of technological solutionism." LSE Public Lecture, March 21. London.

Mosco, Vincent. 2004. *The digital sublime: Myth, power and cyberspace*. Cambridge, MA: MIT Press.

Mouton, Andre. 2013. "Social networks: Building empires, not businesses." *USA Today*. Retrieved April 1, 2013 (http://www.usatoday.com/story/tech/2013/04/01/social-networks-minyanville/2041801)

Nakamura, Lisa. 2002. *Cybertypes: Race, dthnicity, and identity on the Internet*. New York: Routledge.

Nastasi, Alison. 2010. "An update on 'The Star Wars Kid.'" MovieFone.com. Retrieved June 3, 2010 (http://blog.moviefone.com/2010/06/03/an-update-on-the-star-wars-kid)

Nissenbaum, Helen. 2009. *Privacy in context: Technology, policy, and the integrity of social life*. Palo Alto, CA: Stanford University Press.

NPR. 2010. "Student's suicide highlights bullying over sexuality." NPR.org. Retrieved September 30, 2010 (http://www.npr.org/templates/story/story.php?storyId=130242650)

Nye, David. 2006. *Technology matters: Questions to live with*. Cambridge, MA: MIT Press.

Omand, Sir David, Jamie Bartlett, and Carl Miller. 2012. "Introducing social media intelligence (SOCMINT)." *Intelligence and National Security 27*(6): 801–23.

O'Reilly, Tim. 2005. "What is Web 2.0: Design patterns and business models for the next generation of software." Retrieved September 30, 2005 (http://oreilly.com/web2/archive/what-is-web-20.html)

Papacharissi, Zizi. 2002. "The virtual sphere: The Internet as public sphere." *New Media and Society 4*(1): 9–27.

——— 2009. "The virtual geographies of social networks: A comparative analysis of Facebook, LinkedIn and ASmallWorld." *New Media & Society 11*(1, 2): 199–220.

Parker, Ian. 2012. "The sory of a suicide: Two college roommates, a webcam, and a tragedy." *The New Yorker.* Retrieved February 6, 2012 (http://www.newyorker.com/reporting/2012/02/06/120206fa_fact_parker?currentPage=all)

Pew. 2012. "Facebook: A profile of its 'friends.'" Pew Internet Blog. Retrieved May 16, 2012 (http://pewinternet.tumblr.com/post/23177613721/facebook-a-profile-of-its-friends-in-light-of)

Poster, Mark. 1995. *The second media age.* Cambridge: Polity Press.

Powers, Thomas. 2003. "Real wrongs in virtual communities." *Ethics and Information Technology 5*(4): 191–98.

Protalinski, Emil. 2012. "Are teens ditching Facebook for Twitter?" ZDNet. Retrieved January 30, 2012 (http://www.zdnet.com/blog/facebook/are-teens-ditching-facebook-for-twitter/8191)

Reputation. 2012. "Reputation defender: Fix your Google results today." Reputation.com. Accessed online at http://www.reputation.com/reputationdefender

Rheingold, Howard. 1993. *The virtual community: Homesteading on the electronic frontier.* Cambridge, MA: MIT Press. Accessed online at http://www.rheingold.com/vc/book/intro.html

Richtel, Matt. 2012. "Young, in love and sharing everything, including a password." *The New York Times.* Retrieved January 17, 2012 (http://www.nytimes.com/2012/01/18/us/teenagers-sharing-passwords-as-show-of-affection.html)

Ringrose, Jessica, Rosalind Gill, Sonia Livingstone, and Laura Harvey. 2012. "A qualitative study of children, young people and 'sexting': A report prepared for the NSPCC." Accessed online at http://www.nspcc.org.uk/inform/resourcesforprofessionals/sexualabuse/sexting-research-report_wdf89269.pdf

Ritzer, George and Nathan Jurgenson. 2010. "Production, consumption, prosumption: The nature of capitalism in the age of the digital 'prosumer.'" *Journal of Consumer Culture 10*(1): 13–36.

Robbins, Benjamin. 2012. "Future mobile—is creepy the new cool?" The *Guardian.* Retrieved September 14, 2012 (http://www.guardian.co.uk/media-network/media-network-blog/2012/sep/14/future-mobile-creepy)

Robinson, Laura. 2007. "The cyber-self: The self-ing project goes online, symbolic interaction in the digital age." *New Media and Society 9*(1): 93–110.

Rohracher, Harald. 2003. "The role of users in the social shaping of environmental technologies." *Innovation: The European Journal of Social Science Research 16*(2): 177–92.

Rosen, Jeffrey. 2012. "The right to be forgotten." *The Atlantic.* Retrieved July, 2012 (http://www.theatlantic.com/magazine/archive/2012/07/the-right-to-be-forgotten/9044)

Satell, Greg. 2013. "How much is Facebook really worth?" Forbes.com. Retrieved February 21, 2013 (http://www.forbes.com/sites/gregsatell/2013/02/21/how-much-is-facebook-really-worth)

Scheff, Thomas J. 2006. *Goffman unbound! A new paradigm for social science*. Boulder, CO: Paradigm Publishers.

Schneider, Christopher and Daniel Trottier. 2012. "The 2011 Vancouver riot and the role of Facebook in crowd-sourced policing." *BC Studies 175*: 93–109.

Schraube, Ernst. 2009. "Technology as materalized action and its ambivalences." *Theory and Psychology 19*(2): 296–312.

Sessions, Lauren F. 2009. "'You looked better on Myspace': Deception and authenticity on Web 2.0." *First Monday 14*(7). Accessed online at http://firstmonday.org/htbin/cgiwrap/bin/ojs/index.php/fm/article/view/2539/2242

Shariff, Shaheen. 2008. *Cyber-bullying: Issues and solutions for the school, the classroom and the home*. New York: Routledge.

Shirky, Clay. 2008. *Here comes everybody: The power of organizing without organizations*. New York: Penguin.

Silverstone, Roger and Leslie Haddon. 1996. "Design and the domestication of information and communication technologies: Technical change and everyday life." Pp. 44–74 in *Communication by design: The politics of information and communication technologies*, ed. Roger Silverstone and Robin Mansell. Oxford: Oxford University Press.

Slater, Don. 1998. "Trading sexpics on IRC: Embodiment and authenticity on the Internet." *Body & Society 4*(4): 91–117.

Slee, Mark. 2008. "Check out the new Facebook." The Facebook Blog. Retrieved July 21, 2008 (https://blog.facebook.com/blog.php?post=23612952130)

Socialbakers. 2012. "New number 1: Asia became the largest continent on Facebook. Accessed online at http://www.socialbakers.com/blog/878-new-number-1-asia-became-the-largest-continent-on-facebook

———— 2013a. "Facebook statistics by contintent." Accessed online at http://www.socialbakers.com/countries/continents

———— 2013b. "Facebook statistics by country." Accessed online at http://www.socialbakers.com/facebook-statistics

Solove, Daniel. 2007a. *The future of reputation: Gossip, rumor, and privacy on the Internet*. New Haven, CT: Yale University Press.

———— 2007b. "'I've got nothing to  hide' and other misunderstandings of privacy." *San Diego Law Review 44*: 745–72.

Spaulding, Pam. 2010. "Why did Tyler Clementi die?" CNN.com. Retrieved October 1, 2010 (http://edition.cnn.com/2010/OPINION/09/30/spaulding.rutgers.suicide)

Spitzer, Robert. 1981. "The diagnostic status of homosexuality in DSM–III: A reformulation of the issues." *American Journal of Psychiatry 138*(2): 210–15.

Stoerger, Sharon. 2009. "The digital melting pot: Bridging the digital native–immigrant divide." *First Monday 14*(6). Accessed online at http://firstmonday.org/htbin/cgiwrap/bin/ojs/index.php/fm/article/view/2474/2243

Stutzman, Fred, Ralph Gross, and Alessandro Acquisti. 2012. "Silent listeners: The evolution of privacy and disclosure on Facebook." *Journal of Privacy and Confidentiality 4*(2), Article 2. Accessed online at http://repository.cmu.edu/jpc/vol4/iss2/2

Tapscott, Don. 1998. *Growing up digital: The rise of the Net generation.* New York: McGraw-Hill.

Thomas, William I. 1923. *The unadjusted girl. With cases and standpoint for behavior analysis.* Boston, MA: Little, Brown and Co.

Thomas, William I. and Dorothy Swaine Thomas. 1928. *The child in America: Behavior problems and programs.* New York: Knopf.

Toma, Catalina and Jeffrey Hancock. 2010. "Looks and lies: The role of physical attractiveness in online dating self-presentation and deception." *Communication Research 37*(3): 335–51.

Topping, Alexandra. 2012. "Social networking sites fuelling stalking, report warns smartphones and social networking sites are making it much easier for stalkers to target victims, say charities." The *Guardian*. Retrieved February 1, 2012 (http://www.guardian.co.uk/technology/2012/feb/01/social-media-smartphones-stalking)

Trottier, Daniel. 2012a. "Interpersonal surveillance on social media." *Canadian Journal of Communication 37*(2): 319–32.

——— 2012b. *Social media as surveillance: Rethinking visibility in a converging world.* Farnham: Ashgate.

——— (2013) "The business of conversations: Market social media surveillance and visibility." *First Monday 18*(2).

Turkle, Sherry. 1995. *Life on the screen: Identity in the age of the Internet.* New York: Simon & Schuster.

Twitter. 2012. "Welcome to Twitter." Accessed online at http://www.twitter.com

Valdes, Manuel. 2012. "Job seekers getting asked for Facebook passwords: Resume, references, password: Job seekers get asked in interviews to provide Facebook logins." Yahoo! Finance. Retrieved March 20, 2012 (http://finance.yahoo.com/news/job-seekers-getting-asked-facebook-080920368.html)

van Deursen, Alexander and Jan van Dijk. 2011. "Internet skills and the digital divide." *New Media and Society 13*(6): 893–911.

Van Zoonen, Liesbet. 2001. "Desire and resistance: Big Brother and the recognition of everyday life." *Media Culture & Society 23*(5): 669–77.

Wacjman, Judy. 1991. *Feminism confronts technology.* Cambridge: Polity Press.

Wagner, Birgit, Christine Knaevelsrud, and Andreas Maercker. 2006. "Internet-based cognitive-behavioral therapy for complicated grief: A randomized controlled trial." *Death Studies 30*(5): 429–53.

Walker, Joseph. 2012. "Meet the new boss: Big data." The *Wall Street Journal*. Retrieved September 20, 2012 (http://online.wsj.com/article/SB10000872396390443890304578006252019616768.html)

Warren, Samuel and Louis D. Brandeis. 1890. "The right to privacy." *Harvard Law Review 15*(5).

Watkins, S. Craig. 2009. *The young and the digital: What the migration to social-network sites, games, and anytime, anywhere media neans for our future.* Boston, MA: Beacon Press.

Weiser, Mark. 1991. "The computer for the twenty-first century." *Scientific American*, September: 94–104.

Wellner, Alison Stein. 2005. "U.S. attitudes toward interracial dating are liberalizing." *Population Research Bureau*, June, 2005. Accessed online at http://www.prb.org/Articles/2005/USAttitudesTowardInterracialDatingAreLiberalizing.aspx

Westin, Alan. 1967. *Privacy and freedom*. New York: Atheneum.

White, Michelle. 2003. "Too close to see: Men, women, and webcams." *New Media and Society 5*(1): 7–28.

Whitson, Jennifer and Kevin D. Haggerty. 2008. "Identity theft and the care of the virtual self." *Economy and Society 37*(4): 572–94.

Whitty, Monica. 2008. "Revealing the 'real' me, searching for the 'actual' you: Presentations of self on an internet dating site." *Computers in Human Behavior 24*(4): 1707–23.

Winner, Langdon. 1986. *The whale and the reactor: A search for limits in an age of high technology*. Chicago, IL: University of Chicago Press.

Wired. 2003. "Star Wars kid files lawsuit." Wired.com. Retrieved July 24, 2003 (http://www.wired.com/culture/lifestyle/news/2003/07/59757)

Wittel, Andreas. 2001 "Toward a network sociality." *Theory, Culture and Society 18*(6): 51–76.

Wood, David. 2006. "A report on the surveillance society for the information commissioner by the Surveillance Studies Network." Accessed online at http://www.ico.gov.uk/upload/documents/library/data_protection/practical_application/surveillance_society_full_report_2006.pdf

Wresch, William. 1996. *Disconnected: Haves and have-nots in the Information Age*. New Brunswick, NJ: Rutgers University Press.

Wykes, Maggie and Barie Gunter. 2005. *The media and body image: If looks could kill*. London, Sage.

Zhao, Shanyang, Sherri Grasmuck, and Jason Martin. 2008. "Identity construction on Facebook: Digital empowerment in anchored relationships." *Computers in Human Behavior 24*(5): 1816–36.

Zimmer, Michael. 2008. "The externalities of Search 2.0: The emerging privacy threats when the drive for the perfect search engine meets Web 2.0." *First Monday 13*(3). Accessed online at http://firstmonday.org/htbin/cgiwrap/bin/ojs/index.php/fm/article/view/2136/1944

Zuckerberg, Mark. 2006. "Calm down. Breathe. We hear you." The Facebook Blog. Retrieved September 6, 2006 (https://blog.facebook.com/blog.php?post=2361295213 0)

Zwilling, Marty. 2013. "Startups must adapt to new customer buying dynamics." *Huffington Post*. Retrieved March 22, 2013 (http://www.huffingtonpost.com/marty-zwilling/startups-must-adapt-to-ne_b_2929052.html)

# Glossary/Index

Note: Page numbers followed by 'f' refer to figures.

**A**

adolescence online 17–18, 27–28

advertising *see* **social advertisements**

**alt:** a group of communities on Usenet that catered to alternative cultures and tastes 11

anonymous identities 10, 13

**audience:** a collection of individuals who witness a social performance 2, 4, 5–6, 8–9, 14, 15, 16, 17–18

**B**

babies online 26–27

**back stage:** a location where a social performance can be managed. Often the performance is suspended in the back stage. 5, 8, 37

Berners-Lee, Tim 11–12

blogs 28

bodies online 8, 29

bullying 26, 28

**C**

Cacnio, Camille 34–35

chat rooms 11, 12, 13, 18

children's digital presence 26–27

*Classmates.com* 28

Clementi, Tyler 1, 2, 33

college life 1, 2, 28–29

**contextual privacy:** an understanding of privacy that binds specific information to specific contexts. This is an alternative to a binary understanding of privacy. 37

# D

death and dying 31

deletion protocol 44

digital divide 36

**digital immigrant:** an individual who was not socialized in a digital media society. Sometimes refers to people born approximately before 1980. 26

**digital media:** devices and software that are used to send and receive information 1–2

challenging online/offline distinction 16, 43

culture and Facebook 3–4

and dissolution of personal/professional barrier 36

potential for civic engagement through 41–42

privacy issues 37–38

risks in using 25–26

social constructivist approach applied to 20

user population 26

**digital native:** an individual who was socialized in a digital media society. Sometimes refers to people born approximately after 1980, although this is debatable. 26

**digital stigma:** a process whereby discrediting personal information is communicated on digital media 1–3

in adolescence and high school 17–18, 27–28

as babies 26–27

caveats in discussion of 2–3, 40–42

at college 1, 2, 28–29

coping with 3, 33–34, 36–37, 42–44

death and dying 31

deletion protocol to potentially remedy 44

at different life stages 25–32

incidence of 35–36

job applications and retention 30–31

mistaking a social problem for an individual concern 42

new technology opportunities for 42–44

overcoming 35

party photographs and 8, 20, 28, 35, 36

romance and relationships 29–30

sharing of personal information contributing to 15

short and long-term consequences 34–35

social constructivist approach to 20

from stigma to 7–9

**discreditable:** an individual who possess a stigma that, although not immediately visible, has the potential to cause embarrassment 33

**discredited:** an individual who possesses a stigma that is visible, and as such causes embarrassment 33

**dramaturgy:** a framework that understands social relations as performances, complete with roles, stages, and audiences 5–7, 8–9

**E**

embarrassment, online 6, 9, 29, 33, 35, 39

**F**

Facebook 1–2
    and digital media culture 3–4
    employers' searching on 31
    function creep 24
    harming a reputation on 17–18
    long-term predictions for 23, 27
    penetration rate 3f
    privacy settings 2–3, 20, 37, 38
    profiles 14
    wall 22
falsified stigmas 28

**front stage:** a location where a social performance takes place 5, 7, 8, 29, 37, 39

**function creep:** a process by which a technology that is used and accepted in one context is then used in a separate context 24

**G**

**geolocation:** a feature of digital media that locates an individual based on information that they submit 43

**given information:** information that is explicitly communicated during a social interaction 5

**given-off information:** information that is implicitly communicated during a social interaction (ex: body language) 5

**Goffman, Erving:** Canadian-born sociologist who is credited with introducing dramaturgical analysis. His most recognized works include *Presentation of Self in Everyday Life* (1959) and *Stigma* (1963). 4–7, 15, 33–34

Google 8, 13, 34

**H**

Harry, Prince 28–29
high school online 27–28

# I

identity freedom and early web 10–13

institutions 4, 7, 17–18

Internet

blurring of offline/online distinction 16, 43

early 8, 10, 11–12, 39

removing content from 44

shame 34–35, 41

user population 26, 36

**Internet Relay Chat:** an Internet protocol used for exchanging text. Was a popular communication service prior to social media. 11

*isanyoneup.com* 29

# J

job applications 8, 30–31, 44

# L

LinkedIn 4, 20, 30

location privacy 43

**long-term data collection:** a social condition where an individual routinely submits personal information to social media and other online platforms over a prolonged period of time 43–44

# M

mass media, use of user-generated content 14

**memorializing:** a process by which a recently deceased individual's profile is transformed, such that it becomes suitable for collective mourning 31

mobile phones 19, 20, 22, 28

**mobile web:** the ability to access the Internet via a portable device, such as a cellular phone 16

**moral career:** a process by which a stigmatized individual learns how to cope with their stigma 33

mutual shaping 20–24

**Myspace angle:** the process of taking a photograph in a deliberately flattering angle, often with the intention of posting this photograph online 29

# N

networked publics 21

nonymous identities 15

**O**

online dating 29–30

**own:** an individual who experiences the same stigma as somebody else 33

**P**

party photographs 8, 20, 28, 35, 36

**passing:** a social strategy where individuals uphold a shared reality by concealing and implicitly denying the existence of stigmatizing attributes 6–7, 26

**postmodernism:** a perspective in the social sciences that questions the progressive nature of modern societies 10

**privacy:** an individual right to be shielded from exposure, or to be excluded. In the context of digital media, privacy refers to the right to withhold personal information. 7, 19, 37–38, 41–42, 43

    *see also* **contextual privacy**

    Facebook privacy settings 2–3, 20, 37, 38

    location 43

profiles 14

prosumption 13, 21

pseudonymous identities 13, 15

**R**

Raza, Ghyslain 35

reality television programs 37–38

relationships 29–30

**reputation:** an individual's social standing 1

    building and sustaining a 6–7

    on early web 12–13

    harming of a person's 2, 4, 7, 17–18, 34–35

    impacting peers' 28, 30, 35–36, 38

    managing an online 2, 8, 9, 23, 26, 35–36

    memorial pages and 31

    specific effects of technologies on 18–19

*Reputation.com* 8, 26

**revenge website:** a website where individuals are encouraged to submit embarrassing and often sexually explicit content about other individuals 30

riots 34–35

**S**

**sexting:** the act of sending sexually explicit text, images, and video to another individual via a cellular phone 28

shame 6, 30, 34, 41
  and post-shame culture 37–38
**sharing:** the act of making personal information available to others on social media
  platforms 14–15, 16, 27
**social advertisements:** online advertisements that are customized based on personal
  information that is collected about the individual recipient 42–43
**social constructionism:** a perspective in the social sciences that treats social
  phenomena as the product of social actors' shared beliefs and intentions 17, 19–20,
  21, 40
social convergence 12, 15, 26
**social media:** a series of web-based communication platforms that rely on user-
  generated content 1, 2, 9, 15–16, 23
  recent scholarship on 21–22
**spoiled identity:** an individual identity that has been tarnished as a result of
  stigmatizing information 7
  at different life stages 25–32
  living with 33–38
  potential on early web for 12–13
Star Wars Kid 35
**stigma:** a social attribute that labels an individual as shameful and undesirable. In
  his study of stigma, Goffman identifies three types of social stigma including
  abominations of the body, blemishes of character, and tribal stigmas. 6
  concealing stigmatized information 6–7, 26
  coping with 33–34
  falsified 28
  from stigma to digital stigma 7–9
  tribal 6, 8
  visible 6, 33


**T**
**technological determinism:** a perspective in the social sciences that emphasizes the
  extent to which technologies shape our social world 17, 18–19, 21
technologies, new
  common trajectory in introduction of 23
  deletion protocol 44
  geolocation 43
  mutual shaping of 20–24
  problem of long-term data collection 43–44
  social advertising on digital media platforms 42–43
  and social constructionism 19–20
  social impact of 17–24

and social problems 18, 19, 42

and technological determinism 18–19

tensions with 17–18

Twitter 2, 14, 27

## U

*Unbaby.me* 27

**Usenet:** a popular online community that was used extensively in the 1980s and 1990s 11, 13

**user-generated content:** information that individual users submit to online platforms. This typically includes personal information. 13–15

## V

Vancouver riots 2011 34–35

**viral content:** online content that spreads to a large amount of individuals in a small period of time 8, 17, **35**

## W

web

identity freedom and early 10–13

late 16

**Web 2.0:** a term that refers to a series of online trends that emerged in the early 21st century, including a rise in user-generated content. This term has largely been supplanted by the term social media. 13–16

**wise:** an individual who does not experience stigma, but is aware of and sympathetic to a specific kind of stigma 33

## Y

YouTube 14, 27

# Custom Materials
## DELIVER A MORE REWARDING EDUCATIONAL EXPERIENCE.

**University Readers®**
Custom Publishing Evolved.

**Routledge**
Taylor & Francis Group

## The Social Issues Collection

This unique collection features 250 readings plus 45 recently added readings for undergraduate teaching in sociology and other social science courses. The social issues collection includes selections from Joe Nevins, Sheldon Elkand-Olson, Val Jenness, Sarah Fenstermaker, Nikki Jones, France Winddance Twine, Scott McNall, Ananya Roy, Joel Best, Michael Apple, and more.

**1** Go to the website at routledge.customgateway.com

**2** Choose from almost 300 readings from Routledge & other publishers

**3** Create your complete custom anthology

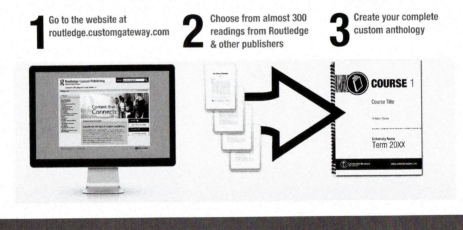

## Learn more:
### routledge.customgateway.com | 800.200.3908 x 501 | info@cognella.com

University Readers is an imprint of Cognella, Inc. ©1997-2013

WITHDRAWN
HOWARD COUNTY LIBRARY

CPSIA information can be obtained at www.ICGtesting.com
Printed in the USA
LVOW01s1712191015

458857LV00008B/255/P

9 780415 643450